NEIL SIMPSON has been a staff reporter on the *Daily Mirror*, *Sunday Telegraph* and *Mail on Sunday* as well as writing for various newspapers and magazines. His recent books include *Gordon Ramsay: The Biography*, *Charlotte Church: Hell's Angel*, *Jade: Story of a Survivor* and *Kings of Comedy: The Biography of Matt Lucas and David Walliams*.

PAUL O'GRADY
THE BIOGRAPHY

NEIL SIMPSON

JOHN BLAKE

Published by John Blake Publishing Ltd,
3 Bramber Court, 2 Bramber Road,
London W14 9PB, England

www.blake.co.uk

First published in paperback in 2008

ISBN: 978 1 84454 577 3

British Library Cataloguing-in-Publication Data:

A catalogue record for this book is available from the British Library.

Design by www.envydesign.co.uk

Printed in the UK by CPI Bookmarque, Croydon, CR0 4TD

3 5 7 9 10 8 6 4 2

Papers used by John Blake Publishing are natural, recyclable products made
from wood grown in sustainable forests. The manufacturing processes
conform to the environmental regulations of the country of origin.

Every attempt has been made to contact the relevant copyright-holders, but
some were unobtainable. We would be grateful if the appropriate people
could contact us.

Contents

INTRODUCTION
Live At Five

It is easy to miss the car with the dark windows as it heads west from Tower Bridge towards the London Eye. It's easy to ignore it as it snakes along the roads beside the Thames and pulls up alongside The London Studios, the high rise building that was once called the LWT Tower. At first glance it can be equally easy to overlook the tall, thin and ordinary-looking figure that pulls himself out of the back seat. But if you are close enough to hear the rasping Liverpool accent as the passenger shares a final joke with his driver then there is no mistaking his identity. Paul O'Grady has arrived at work. And in many ways it feels as if he is coming home.

Paul always smiles as he darts from the car to the studio door. It was in the vast studios of the south bank that a star-struck Paul first watched his showbusiness heroes and heroines perform. It was in the same studios that he would ultimately join the entertainment elite as Lily Savage. Today it is where he can finally be himself as the host of the award-winning *The Paul O'Grady Show*. It is impossible to relax completely with an hour of live television to film. But for Paul there is nowhere on earth he would rather be.

It helps that he has so many old friends amongst his colleagues. And that so many of the same faces keep turning up in his audience. Andy Collins, his long-standing warm-up man, is normally the first to recognise the regulars. Andy's job is to make sure the audience is relaxed, happy and ready for the main event. It has to be one of the easiest jobs in television – because Paul's audiences are always desperate to see the star.

'Okay, everyone. He's going to be here in a minute. Are we ready for him?' That's what Andy normally shouts out after joking with the fans as the black-clad production staff rush around the set making sure everything is ready for the broadcast. A huge cheer always tells Andy that he's got nothing to worry about. On the other side of the plywood set Paul stands and soaks up the atmosphere. He takes a deep breath as the make-up artist does her final checks on his face and hair. It's almost 5pm and Britain's favourite teatime television show is about to go live.

'It's time to go crazy. Knock yourselves out and have fun!' yells Andy as the theme tune begins to play. But the audience hardly needs reminding. Two hundred excited and noisy people are sitting ten deep in the studio. Andy has had everyone in tears of laughter from the moment the doors opened 20 minutes earlier. But it's Paul the fans have really come to see.

The cheering begins again as soon as the opening credits appear on the twelve main television screens suspended from the studio gantries. The foot stamping starts when the day's guests are announced and the theme music fades. And people really do seem ready to knock themselves out when Paul finally appears at the doorway to his set.

Taller, thinner and perhaps a little greyer than many first-timer audience members might expect, Paul looks up at the ten rows of seats, mouth open wide in a huge smile. He stretches his arms out to soak in the welcome, takes a bow and tries to be heard above the racket. Two minutes ago Andy had been worrying that the fans might be too quiet. Now he is behind the cameras trying to calm everyone down.

Insiders say that Channel 4's *The Paul O'Grady Show* has been a television phenomenon – and not just because of the millions of viewers who watch it at home. An extraordinary hardcore of fans try to be at as many recordings as possible, often arriving at the studios up to two hours before the advertised start time to ensure they get a good seat. For the shows that are pre-recorded just after lunch for one of the following afternoons, some three-dozen fans are often turned away when the studio reaches its capacity. For the live shows as many as 100 fans can be turned away.

'The first time I came the ticket said: "Doors open at

4.30pm", so that was when I arrived,' says Paul O'Grady super-fan Carole Roberts who first started turning up when the show was filmed at the BBC studios in West London. 'I didn't get in and realised that that's actually the time you need to be through security and safely inside the centre. When I got my next ticket I arrived an hour before the "Doors Open" time and I was still among the last people to make it in.'

Carole and her fellow fans have now graduated to the yellow-tagged 'priority' tickets, which can attract fierce bidding wars when they become available on internet sites such as ebay. And as often as possible she joins the surprisingly diverse audiences who want to see Paul perform in the flesh. Groups of middle aged women dominate – but they are joined by beautiful twenty-something women with flawless make-up, flash City boys with Louis Vuitton briefcases, hip-looking students out for a good time and pensioners just wanting a laugh in the afternoon.

'We come because Paul is just such a fantastic entertainer,' says Essex-based Jean Lewis, who regularly spends nearly two hours getting to the studios. 'He's funnier and more relaxed off camera than he is when he's being filmed. There are no airs and graces about him and he's always ready to tell jokes at his own expense.' Jean says some of the funniest stories are told during the commercial breaks when Paul's microphone is still turned on. Then he talks about what's in the news, what he did the previous day, whatever comes into his heard first. She says Paul is always happy to laugh away with the audience while his production team fuss around moving the props, touching up his make-up and preparing for the next part of the show.

On or off camera it is the brilliant anecdotes about his life and the endless stream of trenchant opinions on the world in general that keep Paul's fans coming back for more. They are also the reason why Channel 4 was so keen to win the show from ITV back in 2006 – and why it is so important to its schedules for 2008 and beyond.

But for all those anecdotes and observations, the real story of Paul's incredible life has never really been told. Millions of fans have heard plenty of stories and gathered many nuggets of information. But the full picture is only now coming together – and it's as astonishing as the man himself. Friends and confidants say that the Paul O'Grady that the fans don't really know is the one who sat openmouthed as a boy at some of the wildest parties that Birkenhead had ever seen. The one who ran wild and enjoyed lemonade cider as a child in Ireland. The one who won prizes for boxing and partied harder than any of his friends when they left school and had some spare cash in their pockets. Those in his inner circle talk of Paul O'Grady the traveller, the carer, the father, the husband, the lover.

Then there's the Paul O'Grady who was nearly sick with fear before he first went on stage in a rough south London bar a thousand midnights ago. The Paul who worked so hard and struggled for so long before proving himself as a full-time entertainer. The one who broke down so many barriers and faced so many refusals as he tried to make it into the mainstream. The chain-smoking clubber who has ended up as a modern-day country squire. Today Paul is both a godfather and a grandfather. But he is also something more. Far from the media glare, Paul is also one of the most loyal and protective friends anyone could have. Former *Holby City* actress Amanda Mealing has known Paul for more than 20 years and has valued every moment. 'He has always looked out for me, always been very protective of me. He's been consistent and he's been loyal, which is pretty rare for people in this business. He is the one who is always there at two o'clock in the morning when I need someone to talk to. That's what makes a true friend,' she says proudly.

The singer Sonia, the former stand-up star Brenda Gilhoohy and presenter Gaby Roslin also attest to how supportive Paul can be when other peoples' careers take something of a dip. If he can help out by asking them on to one of his shows, then he will. And if he can show support by appearing alongside them on one of their shows, then that's what he will do.

And while his friendships with the likes of Cilla Black and Barbara Windsor are now well documented, Paul has formed bonds with other much less likely names. The fierce *Sun* columnist Garry Bushell might not seem like an obvious fan of a louche former drag artist, but Garry says the longer he knows Paul, the more he respects him. 'He's the sort of bloke everyone warms to,' he admits.

And Paul is also the sort of bloke who won't let

convention stand in the way when those he love are in need. 'He's a wonderful friend. When I lost my hair he offered to lend me one of Lily's wigs,' says former Northern Ireland Secretary Mo Mowlam, who suffered from jibes from the press about her hair loss before revealing it was due to treatment for a brain tumour. Mowlam, who died in 2005, knew Paul for nearly two decades – though she turned down his wig offer, thinking the House of Commons was not quite ready for a cast-off from the bombshell from Birkenhead.

'Thank you everybody, thank you, thank you.' In 2008 and back at The London Studios, Paul always gives a big final wave to the audience as he and his guests disappear backstage at the end of the show. However easy and effortless it might appear, Paul always says a silent prayer of thanks whenever he makes it through the hour without any disaster. And he always knows that everything could have fallen flat if the fans hadn't been having fun. 'I just want the show to be like a party, a group of pals gabbing away about the first things that come into their heads. There are always enough things in life to worry and get depressed about. I want my show to take our minds off all that stuff, even if it's only for a while,' he says. That ability to focus on the good times and enjoy life while you can is now deeply ingrained in Paul's character. It is something he watched as a small boy in a street full of grafters, chancers and survivors. It is a lesson he learned during his long, tough years as a social worker. It has been a fact of his life as tragedy and illness have struck family and friends alike. Ultimately it is a gift he was given all those years ago back in Birkenhead.

CHAPTER ONE

The Boy from Birkenhead

'The Irish families in Liverpool always had the biggest parties and made the most noise,' says Cilla Black, who grew up alongside whole streets of them in the 1950s. Paul O'Grady, later to become one of Cilla's closest friends, could certainly vouch for her story.

Paul James O'Grady was born the youngest of three children into one of those big, noisy extended families on 13 June, 1955. The O'Gradys lived in a three-bed semi in Birkenhead, one of the toughest of Liverpool's working-class districts. And from the start it was the ultimate crowded house. Alongside his mum, dad, elder sister Shelagh and much older brother Brendan, a selection of aunts, uncles, cousins and friends seemed to be with the O'Grady clan almost full-time. Neighbours also took full advantage of the family's open door policy,

1

coming round early in the morning to borrow something from the kitchen and ending up staying all day. Gossip, jokes and wisecracks abounded and Paul was centre of attention from the start. Born more than ten years after his sister, this late miracle baby was passed endlessly from arm to arm as the women gossiped and the men told tall tales of the seas.

Most of the men in those days worked for the Merchant Navy and were away for several weeks at a time – triggering massive, rowdy celebrations whenever they returned. Paul has loved a party ever since and as a boy he was already in his element. 'I grew up loving the days we had a keg of beer in the kitchen and a party all over the house,' Paul remembers. 'At that age I'd never been in a proper bath, let alone in a boat. But water and the sea were utterly alluring to me. I lapped up all the men's stories about monkeys and bushbabies and exotic places. These men were the best storytellers in the world. They were instinctively good entertainers and they taught me how to let my own imagination run riot.'

The men also taught the baby of the family that there was nothing wrong with showing your emotions. He would watch enthralled as the tears started to flow just as fast as the beer. 'My dad in particular was very emotional. He was a typical Irishman who would cry at the drop of a hat,' says Paul, who has certainly followed in his father's footsteps. Recently he joked that he needed help getting off a plane after sobbing uncontrollably through the in-flight movie – the cartoon version of *Tarzan*.

This ability to be in touch with his feelings wasn't the only lesson Paul learned from his father. Paddy, born and raised as a farmer in Galway, had surprising depths and strong beliefs. He had shocked his own family a generation ago when he had enlisted in the RAF in England during the Second World War and left Ireland behind for good. He did it because he believed that the war in Europe had to be fought. He felt that Hitler and fascism had to be beaten. And he hated that Ireland had decided to stay neutral in what he thought was the most important moral battle of the century. Paddy's unspoken message was simple. Whatever the costs, you have to stay true to yourself and stand up for what you believe. It was a message his youngest son received loud and clear and never forgot.

So while money was tight and times could be hard, Paul says family life was as good as it could be. 'I never once saw my mum and dad fight, and when I look back on my childhood I have no bad memories,' Paul says. 'Our family was loving and full of affection. I never knew what divorce was until I moved to London. I was an indulged child and completely protected from anything bad.'

He was also given a front-row seat for some of the best entertainment in town. 'All the comedy I know I learned as a child in Birkenhead,' he said years later. 'The wise-cracking uncles and the colourful aunts were wonderful. Those women were just fabulous. They were salt of the earth types who smelt of last night's scent with too much make-up and mules that went "clack, clack, clack" on the floor.'

Without realising it at the time, Paul was surrounded by a thousand Lily Savages, not least his extraordinary Auntie Chrissie, one of the city's toughest and mouthiest bus conductors. 'She was very Lily,' Paul would say years later. 'Fag in the gob, head full of rollers and never left you without a one-liner. You had to be quick with Auntie Chrissie.'

You had to be just as fast with his mum Molly's dry, cutting humour and with the caustic wit of his other favourite Auntie Annie. It was Annie who made Paul laugh so much that he cried when she told the story of the real life bushbaby her husband had supposedly brought back from his time on the seas one year. Soft, quiet and adorable by day, everyone had forgotten that bushbabies are nocturnal. 'It was fine when it was light, of course, but when my Auntie Annie went to bed it wrecked the house,' Paul says. What no one remembers is what happened to it – a family secret that Paul jokes may one day shame them all.

As a boy, the other things Paul desperately hoped the sailors would have in their bags were the gaudy American comics he had fallen in love with. He would sit for hours poring over the pictures, dreaming about the characters and the settings. He would wonder if one day he too would get to see the American streets first-hand. His sister Shelagh says Paul was a surprisingly good cartoonist himself, starting off by copying pictures from his latest acquisition and then drawing whole new pictures and storylines of his own. 'Paul was talented but he was a very normal, ordinary little boy, no different to anybody else,' she says. But the extraordinary imagination that would one day give birth to Lily Savage was already starting to become apparent.

Christmas was always a good example. Every year the staunchly Roman Catholic family would put a nativity set in the lounge and Paul would send the Three Wise Men on a bizarrely unconventional journey. They would go all around the house until the big day, creating whole narratives to explain each part of their trek. 'One day they would be on the stairs, the next in the loo, the next the hall,' he says. But in one of his favourite memories he says Auntie Chrissie destroyed the magic in typical Lily Savage fashion.

'Ya bastard, I'll kill you!' she yelled at the eight-year-old Paul, after nearly breaking her leg tripping over one of the Magi on the stairs.

'But they're travelling on their way to the manger,' he told her.

'They're from Woolies!' she screamed, bursting his bubble and storming out of the house.

As if the larger than life characters of Birkenhead weren't enough for Paul, he had plenty of new ones to observe during the summer school holidays when he was packed off to stay with his dad's family in Ireland, as his parents couldn't get enough time off work to look after their youngest son. And he thrived on the boat journey from Liverpool to Dublin and then the train trip to Castlereagh, where the real entertainment would begin.

There were no rules about children going in to pubs back then, and Paul loved drinking lemonade cider and listening to what the adults said and how they said it. The way older people talked already fascinated him. He couldn't believe how fast their minds could leap from subject to subject, how quickly they could come up with a joke, a put-down or a whole new anecdote. Paul also loved the fantastic characters he met in Ireland, not least his wonderful Auntie Bridget who drank poteen, loved wrestling and could swear like a soldier.

It seemed as though everyone in the Irish branch of the O'Grady family owned a pub and Paul reckons he got drunk for the first time on his first Irish summer when he was just eight years old – not least because the youngsters would wander around the bars all night, nicking the Guinness out of the drip trays and trying to swig the dredges of any forgotten pints left around the bars. On other nights, he and his cousins would happily sup Cidona, a kind of cider for kids that he still loves today.

The farm itself where Paul stayed was tiny. Lost in the middle of nowhere in Galway it felt, even then, like going back in time. 'There was no electricity, no lights, no real plumbing, no toilets, and it was a two-bedroom farmhouse with about eleven children in it. I slept on a sofa and had a ball,' Paul remembers.

Today, looking back at old photographs, Paul can't believe how young and healthy he looks. 'I was totally wild, like a gypsy's kid,' he reckons. He and his cousins spent all their days outside, roaming the bog lands, helping the adults cut the turf, devouring huge doorstep butties for lunch and then heading off for another adventure. It was a taste of freedom and a chance to feel grown up while retaining all the benefits of childhood. Once more there were wonderful visitors to the tiny farmhouse – Paul's grandparents had a seemingly vast gang of pals who came round and proved that you didn't have to be in Birkenhead to have a proper party or spin some fantastic stories.

And on his way home at the end of each summer, Paul would beg to be allowed a fried breakfast at the famous Bewley's Café in Dublin's Grafton Street – a place he still rushes back to every time he returns to Ireland.

Back in the three-bed semi in Birkenhead there was one key repercussion from the trip he would make for nearly eight years: the language that Paul would always get into trouble for. The swearing was second nature in Galway, but when Paul effed and blinded at home a few clips round the ear from his parents told him he needed to clean up his act. The other thing Paul got from those summers was an Irish passport. So to this day, Paul James O'Grady can also travel under the name of Padraic Seamus O'Grady, if he so chooses.

Religion was the next big influence in Paul's life. The blond, mop-headed kid was an altar boy, sang in the choir and played a big part in local church life, even though the spiritual side of the services tended to matter less than their sheer theatricality and stagecraft. 'It was all going to church, stations of the cross, novenas, and Union of Catholic Mothers' coach trips to Lourdes, Knock or Pantasa, which was a place Our Lady appeared in Wales,' Paul says. 'She was a very busy woman, Our Lady. She was all over the gaff.'

And it was just as well. Because these visitations triggered vast, noisy charabanc trips that Paul thrived on. 'We'd all go and do our penance and go to church and all that. But basically it was a coach full of mad women and their kids – the kids at the back with the pop, the mums at the front with pale ale. And on the way back someone would always get a bit bevvied and sing *I Get The Blues When It Rains.*'

Once more, Paul was taking everything in. He was watching how these brave and sometimes maudlin women acted, what they said, how they dressed and how they got through their days. He had no idea why it all mattered so much to him, or whether it would ever be useful to him. But still he lapped it all up.

What Paul also loved was the sheer irrationality of many of those around him. He loved his parents for having such strong opinions about life and for letting everything out rather than keeping things inside. So he cheered inwardly when his staunchly republican dad ripped pictures of the royal family out of encyclopaedias and when his mum threw anything she had to hand at the television whenever Ian Paisley appeared on it. He also loved the times when the whole family were laughing like drains at their comedy heroes. To this day, Paul still adores the likes of Frankie Howerd, *Not On Your Nellie* star Hylda Baker and the music hall and radio comedian Robb Wilton. But there is far more to Paul than the indulged child who loved to watch when the adults were being dramatic. At heart he is a true child of Merseyside, so he has always been much tougher than he might have appeared.

When he was ten years old Paul was first taken to boxing training by his dad. By the time he was eleven he had become taller than most of his peers, was winning fights and learning important lessons about how to conduct himself. Even as a grown-up he says the boxing classes gave him confidence – not least because so few people are aware that he ever took them. 'Dad made sure I was no wimp. He was jolly and loving but he was Irish and a tough man, and he did it because he knew it was important.' Paddy was thrilled when his young son won boxing trophies – because he wanted to be certain that Paul would always be able to get out of trouble if required.

Paul's religious upbringing meant that his parents had no problem choosing his secondary school, the boys-only St Anselm's Catholic school on the Wirral. Set up by the Congregation of Christian Brothers in 1933, it had a tough academic focus and Paul did well there. He escaped the attentions of any bullies and had a decent network of friends, including several from the years above him. Careers advice wasn't exactly plentiful but the dreamer in Paul was thinking he should follow the neighbourhood lead and go to sea. That way he could see the world, he thought, having already decided he needed to look beyond the Mersey for adventures.

But for all their emotions and domestic dramas, his parents weren't always keen on dreams. When it came to the world of work they were deeply serious. They told Paul he needed a safe, secure job, ideally with a good pension, which was his mother's pet obsession. While they wanted him to stay at school for as long as possible, the key idea was that he would ultimately work for a company like Shell, where his dad was working, when he left. The thought of breaking free, of becoming an actor or an entertainer, was simply out of the question. It wasn't just that his parents wouldn't have approved; it was also that it wouldn't have occurred to Paul or anyone else to give this gamble a try. There hadn't been any drama classes or acting lessons in his childhood. When the family had stayed at Haven Holidays' caravan parks over several summers, there had been plenty of talent shows on stage. But Paul had never even considered taking part – after all, he was the boy who had won cups for boxing, not singing.

'No one in my family has ever done anything like this,' Paul told a reporter from *The Times* years later. 'It's an old joke but if one of our names was in the paper it was in relation to a minor offence.'

One thing Paul does remember about his childhood is

the first time he ever saw a man dressed as a woman appear on television. It left him completely cold. 'Look at that! It's a man!' However, Paul remembers that his mum screamed out and pointed at the television when the rival to Danny La Rue made his flamboyant appearance. There was never any question that this sparked some latent desire in Paul to follow suit. 'I've never actually liked drag and I'm not a drag artist. I'm a comedian, Lily is my armour,' he would say years later. 'As a kid I was never in my mother's wardrobe, trying on her wedding dress and singing into a hair dryer.'

What he was doing was having fun. By the time the 1970s were underway, Paul had grown into a tall, good-looking teenager with plenty of friends and the gift of the gab. He wanted to see how far it could take him.

Having moved on to study at Birkenhead Technical College, Paul's academic record suffered as he focused more and more on the parties taking place around him. Today he talks about his French O-level and his biology A-level, but he doesn't want to discuss how his other exams went. What he was concentrating on was illustration, and he considered a series of courses at art college. The classic American comics he had been given by neighbours as a boy were still in his room at home and he had subsequently built up a hefty collection of others. But Paul, even then, was a perfectionist. 'If I can't be as good as Walt Disney then there's no point in trying,' he reasoned. And despite more than ten years of drawing practice he knew Walt had nothing to worry about. So Paul set off on some other career adventures – and suffered his fair share of disasters.

A day-release course as a clerical assistant with the Department of Social Security in Birkenhead was one of the latter. 'The course would rot your brain quicker than heroin. It was just dreadful – and I'd not wanted to work for the DSS anyway. I thought I was applying to the Ministry of Defence, and I only wanted to do that because I had some idea that it would be a bit like living in an episode of *The Avengers*,' he told friends.

So what would Paul do with his life? His parents, always so relaxed and supportive, were starting to worry. They kept on plugging away at the idea that he needed a job with a pension, and they pushed him hard until he applied for the job at Shell that had always been his fallback option. At the last minute, though, something told him to steer clear. He deliberately got on the wrong train at Birkenhead station and missed the interview, much to his parents' disgust.

What came next was a wonderful kaleidoscope of part- and full-time jobs ranging from the ridiculous to the sublime. He worked in an abattoir and as an agency cleaner for the likes of local singer Cleo Laine – in that job Paul would arrive at each shift singing 'Don't cry for me, I'm the Cleaner' as a homage to Evita's Elaine Paige and Julie Covington. He chopped wood in a timber yard; he took a £2.50 bus ride down to London to work in a hotel, but was back in Liverpool soon after. Also appearing on his CV, or left as suggestions by his increasingly desperate parents, were manual and white-collar jobs everywhere from the local Vauxhall factory to the massive Cammell Laird shipbuilders. He didn't take up any of the ideas.

The two big jobs that Paul did end up with would both shape his future in different ways and take him through his teenage years into his early twenties. One was as a care assistant in a convalescent home in nearby West Kirby, a tough and emotionally challenging role that Paul coped with by always trying to imagine the patients as they might once have been. He tried not to see them as they were in front of him, damaged by old age, accident or illness. He wanted to feel that they had been grander, greater figures in the past, and his imagination created whole scenarios for them – including a whole cast of supporting characters. When he sat and talked to the patients he would paint detailed pictures in long, rambling anecdotes. The demented, the sedated and the deaf would be his first audiences, and they didn't give much back. But Paul was always happy to let his mind run riot and talk for England as he tried to entertain them. It would stand him in great stead for the future.

The other job that was to influence him was as a magistrates' clerk where a sometimes awestruck Paul really did see all human life parade in front of him. So many of the characters he would create later in his life were born in that courtroom. And it was the women who always caught his eye first.

As a young boy Paul had loved watching westerns, but not really because of the cowboys. He was always waiting for the arrival of the prostitutes: the scenes set in an American brothel presided over by a tough-as-nails madam with a face that had lived a thousand lives. In his Liverpool courtroom, the first real prostitutes Paul had ever seen seemed every bit as powerful and evocative as the characters from those films. Day after day he watched them stand up in court facing minor charges for minor misdemeanours. He says he knew and admired the women the moment he saw them.

'They might have had the rollers ripped out of their hair in the cells but they were so brave. I used to admire them for giving as good as they got,' he said, as yet another shop-lifting or benefit fraud charge was heard. His heart would also break, he says, when he heard about the dull, domestic horrors of their lives, the endless struggles to pay the bills, the constant let-downs from the feckless men. Sitting in the court corridors eating his own lunch, he would listen in on extraordinary conversations about what, for the speakers, were ordinary lives. Strange as it seems, he had never felt more at home.

What made the dawn of the 1970s even better for Paul was that he was also having a ball with all his colleagues. He became thick as thieves with young and old, male and female, new and experienced workers. There were the endless laughs they would have at their desks and in the staff-rooms, and the many scams and secrets they tried to keep from their bosses and the public. And then there were the nights out...

These were wildly social times and as he was still living at home, Paul was prepared to spend every penny of his wages on good times. His network of friends spread far and wide and while he wasn't technically old enough to drink in any pubs and bars, he was still a regular. Glam rock and *The Goodies* were still making everyone laugh and *Monty Python's Flying Circus* was the biggest act around. On the BBC, *The Liver Birds* were making Liverpool cool. They were the best of times to be young, Paul says today.

They were also the very last good times he could enjoy whole-heartedly without worrying about paying any sort of price. He didn't know it at the time, but Paul was about to grow up very, very fast. He was about to learn a lesson that would haunt him for the rest of his life – that you can't have silver linings without black clouds and that fate has a nasty habit of tripping you up just when you think you are on the home straight.

The first evidence of things to come appeared after another night out that Paul enjoyed with his colleagues. He spent most of it sitting with one of the more experienced staff members, Diane Jansen. She was ten years older than Paul and she seemed wildly sophisticated and experienced to her teenage admirer. Suddenly they were kissing, and for a brief period afterwards they would become an item. The office gossips loved it as much as Paul, who was playing scenes from *The Graduate* out in his head before and after every thrilling date. Neither he nor Diane was expecting the relationship to last forever, but in the heady days of the early 1970s they were both having as much fun as possible along the way. Until fate intervened.

'Paul. I'm pregnant.'

The three words hung in the air for so long it was as if time had stood still.

'It will be all right.'

Paul found just five words to say in response. But in truth he had no idea what he was saying or what affect this bombshell would really have on either of their lives. He was still only sixteen years old, with no idea of what bringing up a child would involve. All he wanted was to have fun – and to be free.

Diane was determined to keep her baby – and Paul's own Catholic childhood meant that he didn't even consider suggesting an abortion. But long before the pair worked out how to support their child, Paul knew he had one even bigger hurdle to face. He had to tell his parents what he had done. He had to face what he knew would be both shame and anger. He had to be ready to break their hearts. Night after night Paul tried to pluck up the courage to make the announcement. Every morning he rehearsed how he would tell them. But just when it seemed he had finally found the courage, something happened which would change everything.

In 1973, Molly had a massive heart attack and was

rushed to the local St Catherine's hospital, her whole family following behind the ambulance. Doctors could only give the usual platitudes to the O'Gradys as the woman they all loved was operated on far from their eyes. No one really knew what 'serious but stable' meant. No one really understood all the medical language. But everyone was terrified that the matriarch of their family wouldn't make it through the night. And Paul's dear dad Paddy was beside himself with worry. While no one yet knew it, the scene was set for a family tragedy of extraordinary proportions – a tragedy during which the teenage Paul would be centre stage.

CHAPTER TWO

Breaking Free

The first act of the family tragedy began when Paul and Paddy crept out of the waiting rooms to sit outside and get some fresh air. There was nowhere nice to go. St Catherine's hospital is a former Victorian workhouse, all long corridors, red brick walls and dingy garden areas full of staff and smokers. Paul and his dad joined a group of them as they waited for more news. Neither father nor son really knew what to say as they stared at the brick walls opposite them. They knew they had a long, terrible night ahead and in their own ways they were both trying to build up the strength to cope with it. Then, in almost a whisper, Paddy spoke.

'I can't cope without Molly. I can't live without her.'

'Dad. We're going to be all right.'

Paul remembers how hard he tried to reassure his big,

burly father – the rough, tough Irishman who already seemed a shadow of his former self. Sitting outside the hospital the teenager tried to say that the doctors knew what they were doing, that Molly was in the right place and getting the best possible care. But deep down he knew he wasn't convincing himself, let alone his distraught dad.

So, as the temperature dropped, the pair headed back to the seats in the corridor where they planned to keep vigil for as long as it took to hear that Molly was on the mend. As they approached, Paul remembers his dad leaning against the wall to catch his breath. Then he watched him slide slowly down it. He too had suffered a massive heart attack and he too was rushed to intensive care, to a bed not far from the one occupied by his equally ill wife.

'They told me he wouldn't last the night.' Looking back Paul knows it was right for the doctors to have been so honest with him and the rest of his family. But at the time they were the hardest possible words to hear. Within a matter of hours, the doctors approached the O'Gradys again. Their faces were grave – and no one knew which of their parents must have taken a turn for the worse. As they all stood up, the doctors gave the bad news about Paddy. He had died, despite everyone's efforts to save him.

'The doctors were wonderful and they said that if they could have put the words: "Died of a broken heart" on his death certificate they would have,' Paul says quietly.

It was a sign of the bond between husband and wife, the true love that they had shared for so long, that Paddy simply couldn't conceive of a life on his own. When he had told his young son that he couldn't live a single day without his wife, he had been telling the truth.

And now someone had to tell Molly what had happened.

Paul says he will never forget the sight of his mother, being brought towards them in a wheelchair, wearing her bed jacket and nightie, looking vulnerable and cold in the harsh half-light of the hospital waiting area.

'We've got something to tell you, Molly.'

Paul remembers almost hiding behind a huge cupboard in the room as if this would somehow stop the news being broken. As if this would mean it wasn't true.

There would be more tragedy to come. The doctors said the deeply religious Molly was too ill to attend her husband's funeral, a fact which everyone feared would trigger a relapse and would haunt her for the rest of her life.

And things would never be the same back in Birkenhead when she was finally discharged from hospital, and as she tried to pick up the pieces of life as a widow. She was without her soulmate, feeling alone in even the most crowded rooms. With his brother and sister having long since moved out of the family home, Paul saw more than anyone how hard life was for his mother. He says his heart was broken on so many nights, when he woke at 4am to hear his mother crying out her husband's name. Unable to comfort her, Paul would get on his bike and ride around the streets until her sobbing stopped and it was safe to return. His parents had taught him that love could be a wonderful thing that could last a lifetime. But they had also shown that when tragedy strikes love can tear you apart. On those bleak early mornings as Paul watched dawn break over Birkenhead, he wasn't sure that the love was worth having if the tragedy would always be so close on its heels.

Meanwhile, Diane was growing ever larger, and eventually gave birth to a baby girl. In happier times the idea had been to call her Gypsy Jansen after the famous stripper Gypsy Rose Lee. But in the end, the parents picked the more conventional Sharyn Lee Jansen – and as Paul and Diane were unmarried the baby would never carry the O'Grady name. As he held the baby in his arms, still a teenager himself, Paul knew that everything had changed. And he knew he had to tell his mother what had happened. He had to give her the chance to be a grandmother.

Just as he expected, Molly went berserk – especially when she found out that Diane was much older and should, in her mind, have been more responsible. 'She should know better. An idiot sixteen-year-old like you,' she screamed at her son, as she tried to take in the news. But for all her anger she couldn't hide her humanity. 'I've got to look after her,' Paul remembers his mother repeating again and again, almost to herself, as that long tense afternoon stretched on.

Diane, though, was already getting used to coping on her own. Paul started to give her £3 a week out of his £7 wages but he began to see her less and less often. His mother was also respecting Diane's wishes, even though it meant missing out on her dreams of being a hands-on grandmother. 'I saw Diane and Sharyn on the market today. I spoke to them. She's a lovely little girl.' Paul says his heart broke when his mum told him about a rare chance meeting one day. But deep in his own heart he knew his world had moved on.

At eighteen Paul wanted to be out with his mates rather than in with his baby. Seeing his dad die and his mother struggle with her health had taught him that life could be short. So he felt it had to be enjoyed. The bright lights of Liverpool and London were calling, and as a good-looking lad Paul wanted to chase them. He started to party with fresh vigour and as he did so he began to experiment even more with his sexuality.

The concept of being straight or gay hadn't ever really occurred to him – he had been casually dating both girls and boys as far back as his schooldays without really giving it a second thought. If a pretty girl fancied him and answered his smile, then he would have as much fun as possible with her. If a boy caught his eye, then he would do the same with him. He wasn't making political or social statements. He wasn't really even making many choices – he was just taking advantage of whatever opportunities came his way. For those few carefree years Paul is happy to admit that he was sex mad – almost certifiably so. 'I was having sex with anything that moved, male or female. Even dogs weren't safe, and if it wasn't nailed down I'd have it,' he joked years later. His mum accused him of tom-catting, though Paul says she had little idea of just how broad his list of sexual conquests had become.

Years later Paul realised how compartmentalised this had made his life. As a teenager he had already acquired a dual life: there was the Paul who lived at home and played the good son, and the Paul who went out and partied with the wildest of crowds. What he did at night was his business, he told himself. He was building walls in his life, drawing distinctions and creating different personas for different circumstances. It would be great practice for when Lily Savage needed a life of her own. But in the mid-seventies it wasn't always as easy as it sounds.

The parties he attended and the big nights out had felt legendary at the time, though looking back Paul smiles at the soft, provincial feel of them. One of his gang's favourite ideas was to head out for a big trip down to the hot and sweaty Wigan Casino, the vast soul club that the American *Billboard* magazine said rivalled New York's Studio 54 as one of the best venues in the world. It was a drink-free club, and in an age where drugs were still far from the mainstream, Paul and his friends would take Pro-Plus with a glass of coke to give them the extra buzz they craved. On other nights, they would experiment with Feminax, a medicine designed for period pains that unaccountably made the gang more irritable than excitable.

Could the hedonism have lasted forever? It never does, as Paul now knows. And as the middle of the decade approached, the cracks were already starting to show. The whole country was undergoing a massive recession, with unemployment at its highest levels since the Second World War. Young people were facing futures with little likelihood of ever finding work. Anger and aggression were in the air and Britain was officially seen as the economic basket case of Europe, if not the world. 'Perhaps I should have gone to sea, like I'd planned,' Paul thought to himself. And as the wild boys of Birkenhead all started to look in different directions, Paul was given the chance to do the next best thing. One of his closest pals had announced that he was leaving the country to work in the Philippines. On a whim, at nineteen years old, Paul decided to head East and follow him. It would be the adventure of his life and he had absolutely nothing to lose if it all went wrong.

He turned out to be quite right about the adventures. With no job to go to Paul had to accept pretty much the first thing he could find when he arrived in the Philippines. It would make for some extraordinary memories.

One of his first job offers came from the captain of the fleet of support ships that sailed from Manila to Jakarta to supply the men on the oil rigs. What Paul didn't know when he took the job and set sail on his first voyage, was that modern-day pirates were alive and well and sailing across the South China Sea. Boats full of heavily armed and reckless Chinese bandits were searching for guns, booze and armaments and Paul watched in horror the first few times that his own supply ships were targeted, leaving the captain desperate to explain they had nothing worth stealing.

Despite the dangers, Paul was exhilarated to be following in the footsteps of all the men who had partied so hard at his parents' house throughout his childhood. He was finally able to understand the pressures these sailors had been under. And he loved being able to see first-hand some of the great cities they had talked about so many years ago.

Many of his shore-leave weekends were spent in Hong Kong, though in typical fashion Paul made sure he was introduced to the kind of bars your average tourist or businessman would never find. One of them was Nelson's Bar in what back then was the crowded, intimidating and volatile Wan Chai district. 'It was rough as a dog and westerners weren't normally allowed in. You have to go with some Chinese people and I went with a bunch of oil men. It looked like something out of a movie, choc-full of sailors, gamblers and prostitutes. You needed a bit of bottle to go, but it was my kind of place and I felt at home there,' Paul remembers, glad once more of his height and the boxing training he had gone through as a child.

After tiring of the long supply ship voyages, Paul decided to quit and find work on dry land. Once more, he wasn't in much of a position to be choosy about a job. And once more, he ended up with a classic: as the only western waiter in Gussy's Bar, a club in Manila which doubled up as one of the city's busiest brothels.

As he did in the magistrates' courts in Birkenhead and the low-life bars in Hong Kong, Paul says he felt at home in the brothel. He felt that he belonged, that he knew the rules, the personalities and the stories long before he actually walked through the door.

Some of this strange pre-knowledge might have come from the westerns he had loved as a child – and he was thrilled to see that life was still imitating art. His Hollywood hookers had always had the best lines, worn the best clothes and lived the most dramatic of lives. So too did the women Paul worked with out East. None took any messing from the men who knocked on their doors. And despite the language barrier, Paul says he felt close to them from the start. The place seemed to have the fast, wisecracking atmosphere of his childhood home. He loved it. And as he sat in his tiny apartment on his nights off, writing letters home to his mum, he knew he was learning from it. What he didn't know was when these lessons would ever pay off. Lily Savage was still half a world and what felt like more than a lifetime away. But a tiny part of her had already been formed in Paul's mind.

Moving back to Birkenhead would have been impossible after Paul's adventures in the Far East. So when he eventually came back to Britain there was only one place for him to live: London. The lights were brighter, the bars were busier and the parties louder. Paul joined forces with a rowdy group of his Merseyside friends who were all heading south at the same time. Punk had by now transformed the music scene with the likes of Ian Dury, Blondie, the Boomtown Rats, The Police and Gary Numan competing with the likes of The Clash, the Sex Pistols and Elvis Costello in the charts. Thatcherism was being born, the country was squaring up for big social changes and Paul and his gang vowed to turn the capital upside down.

But while the parties down south would be even wilder than those they had all enjoyed in Birkenhead, Paul was already proving to be more serious than many people had expected. He didn't just live for the wild weekends. He wanted a job that meant something, so he shied away from the easy money in the shops and salons that dominated everyone else's thinking. Instead, he decided to draw on his experience in the convalescent home in West Kirby. He became a care officer with Camden Council. On any count, physical, mental or spiritual, it was one of the toughest jobs in town. The people he met and the scenes he saw would be burnt onto his memory, teaching him lessons about life he could never forget to this day. They taught him that however bleak his own prospects might be, there were always those below him on life's ladder. They taught him, once more, how important it was to root for the underdog.

As he gained experience in his job, one of Paul's

specific roles was to be a near full-time guardian to some of the women and their children in the borough. If ever any of the single mums on his patch had to go into hospital, for example, Paul would often be drafted in to be a temporary surrogate father to their kids. If there was no one else to care for them, he would often move into their homes for days or weeks at a time.

It was a long way from the Birkenhead days, when huge extended families and streets full of good neighbours meant there was always someone there to help out in a crisis. The families Paul dealt with in London often had nothing and no one – if he hadn't been around to step in then many of the kids he looked after would have had to go into care, he says. So, however unconventional his role, he says it always served a better purpose.

At one point Paul looked after six near-abandoned children for almost a year while Social Services looked the other way. Everyone knew that the kids' living conditions were squalid. But everyone also knew that they were safer under Paul's wing than they were in any other situation available to them. So much of his professional life was about compromise and unconventionality. Every case had to be judged on its individual merits with care of the kids trumping any rigid compliance with the rulebook.

One of the many downsides of Paul's job was that he would frequently get abused and punched by angry, irrational fathers who turned up, drunk, at their old homes and assumed he was their former partner's new fancy man. On other occasions he was forced to step in and stop the same drunken fathers from grabbing their children in the middle of the night and taking them off to who knew where to avoid the social workers. Those childhood boxing lessons would once more mean that Paul could easily stand up to these men. But his status and responsibilities as a social worker meant he frequently had to hold back rather than let rip. Often he would be back at his desk at the council trying to explain away a black eye to his equally angry colleagues.

The other awful by-products of Paul's job were the nits and scabies he frequently caught from his young charges. Then there was the horror of finding lonely old people dead and forgotten in their homes when he came round for his regular visits.

'Being a social worker in London at that time was as tough a job as you can possibly imagine,' says former Camden Council officer Leon Best, who followed the same beat as Paul in the 1980s. 'If you were out in the field you would see some sights that could quite literally haunt you. It wasn't the violence or the threats of violence that bothered us the most. It was the fact that you saw so many wasted lives and so many parents whose children would make the same mistakes all over again. Sometimes you really did have to ask why you bothered, why you spent so much energy helping people who couldn't or wouldn't help themselves. Everyone on the council staff had to find their own way of coping with all this and, while it might seem insensitive, there was a lot of gallows humour going on back in the office.'

Paul's other way of getting through his days was to look to the light in even the darkest of situations. It was like his days in the magistrates' court, and he again found himself full of admiration for the way people at the bottom of life's heap managed to cope. He knew many of them brought a huge amount of the bad stuff upon themselves. But if they had spirit and a zest for life he found he could always forgive them for it. 'I met a lot of Lilys back then. London Lilys. They'd say, "I'm just going to the shops, Paul." And then they'd come back three days later. And I couldn't help liking them for it, for seizing their one chance to have a bit of a party.'

He also railed against the rules and the system that he felt stopped him from doing more – and against the way society seemed to make life harder for so many of his charges. 'I wasn't allowed to say that I was heartbroken for people even when I was. I'd sit with a woman who'd had her kids taken off her and we'd have a drink and she'd be saying: "Oh well, they've gone but I'll have a couple more." It was as if she was talking about puppies. I'd go and curse the council and social workers saying: "Give her a break. Educate her." None of the women I knew were vindictive or evil. I knew that inside they were often being ripped to shreds. Circumstances had just got the better of them.'

But while he could forgive the women so much, Paul drew the line at forgiveness when he knew they were being abused by their partners. That, he says, was something he could never excuse or brush away. In the years ahead, this unshakeable belief would show up in his act. 'The women would come back sometimes with black eyes themselves and they'd say it was their fault. I decided right then that Lily would never say that. She wouldn't ever let a fella lay a finger on her. She'd break his arm first, and take great relish in doing so.'

The throwaway comment gave away more than Paul's thoughts on domestic violence. It also revealed that despite his long and sometimes awful days at work he had found room in his life for another very special lady. The regulars at a noisy bar in south London had just been introduced to a certain Lily Savage. They loved her. And Paul was about to embark on the adventure of his life.

CHAPTER THREE

Here's Lily

The bad boys from Birkenhead were still living life to the full as the boom days of the mid-1980s approached. Paul's loosely connected gang of mates were regulars on the pub and club scene across the capital and Paul's problem was finding enough cash to keep up. He didn't get any overtime payments from Camden Council but he did get plenty of time off in lieu of all his unsocial hours. So while most of his mates were necking pints, Paul started to pull them. He worked behind the bars of around half a dozen pubs in his first wild years in London – and met many dozens of equally wild new friends.

After cleaning up at the end of a shift, Paul and the rest of the bar staff would troupe en masse to a late-night venue nearby. Everyone was an expert on

London's underground scene, the rash of gay and gay-friendly clubs that served drinks into the small hours and had lock-ins through until dawn. Heaven, the huge gay nightclub under the arches near Charing Cross Station, had opened in 1979, and was transforming London's reputation as a party city. And anyone from Liverpool was suddenly edgy and cool – Frankie Goes To Hollywood had seen to that – so it still seemed the perfect time to be young, free and single. Or at least it was for most of the O'Grady gang.

'All I'm getting is hassle from my parents for not being married.' One of Paul's closest new friends back then was Portuguese waitress Theresa Fernandes, who Paul had met when they worked behind a bar in London's Bayswater. 'They want me to go back to Portugal but I just can't bear the thought of it,' she said one evening when the friends sat down at the end of a shift.

'I'll marry you, if you want.'

Theresa remembers sitting in shock after Paul made his offer. For a while she thought her new friend was joking. Despite getting on like a house on fire they had only really known each other for a matter of months. And, anyway, by now it was no secret among the London crowd that Paul was gay.

'I'm serious. I'm never going to get married so I'm happy to step in if it'll help you out.'

It might not have been the most romantic of proposals but it didn't seem as if either side had anything to lose by following up on it. So Paul organised the paperwork and marriage certificates while Theresa bought two simple wedding rings. When the licence came through, the bride and groom arrived at the register office in Paddington, west London. Actress Kate Fitzgerald, who had been playing Doreen Corkhill in *Brookside*, was one of the guests. Another of Paul's close friends, Alan Ralph, was best man. The bride wore an off-white suit while the groom was smartly dressed in pale beige.

'Paul had a few brandies but did beautifully,' Theresa says with a smile. 'He even managed to look nervous when I walked up the aisle.'

The wedding party headed out for a boozy afternoon of celebrations – but by the end of the night both Paul and Theresa were back at work behind the bar in Bayswater. Romance might not be dead, Paul joked, but it certainly wasn't making any long-term plans. As it turned out the marriage would last, on paper, for nearly twenty years. It was never consummated, but the pair remained close friends for more than a decade before finally drifting apart. They only got divorced in 2003 – and that was only at the request of Paul's business advisers who were trying to tie up some of the loose ends in their client's financial affairs.

In the 1980s Paul's bed wasn't exactly empty, however. He had met someone who would turn out to be the biggest love, and the greatest influence, on his life. The man's name was Brendan Murphy – Murph or Murphy to Paul and their friends – and he would be at Paul's side almost every day for the next two decades. It would be a love affair as unconventional as anyone who knew Paul might expect – the physical side of it would ultimately disappear to be replaced by an intense spiritual and professional bond. But this unique love affair would have the power, the intensity and the durability to match the connection Paul's parents had enjoyed what felt like a lifetime ago. Tragically, it too would end in an early death.

Looking back, it's hard to see how a character as large as Lily Savage could have found room to grow in Paul's increasingly crowded life. But the imagination that had always run riot in Paul's mind as a child was as powerful as ever. Lily had popped up in that imagination some time ago and true to form she was refusing to leave.

'It was Saturday and Sunday afternoons, play-acting at home with my old friend Alan that she made her first appearance,' Paul remembers. Paul and Alan were huge fans of Victoria Wood and Alan Bennett and would invent an endless series of scenarios for the characters they had created. Characters they had called Lily Savage and Vera Cheesman. One of their favourite ramblings saw the women waiting at home after the funeral of one of their relatives. 'I'd look out of the window as Lily and say: "The cars will be here in a minute, better put the kettle on." And we'd go to the kitchen and start buttering bread,' Paul remembers with a laugh.

On other days, the men would pretend to be factory

workers on sewing machines, taking it in turns to play the supervisor and telling the other one off. It was improv, long before this loose form of comedy really hit the mainstream. For Paul and Alan it was just playing. But for Paul in particular it would prove to be invaluable experience. Lily hadn't yet been seen beyond the reaches of his south London council flat and she was certainly going to go through some radical changes before she made her public debut. But she was now a part of him. She was a real person and he already knew her as well as anyone else in his life.

Working in the bar in Bayswater had been good fun. But in the mid-1980s the really fun gay scene was developing south of the river. A small network of pubs was offering an inspired mix of boozy, cruisy nights and good old-fashioned live entertainment. There were great DJs playing great music. But there were also comedy turns, talent nights, strippers, sing-songs and karaoke. Gay men dominated the crowds, but students, hooray Henries and fashion victims were almost as well represented. A lot of it was kitsch and corny but somehow it all felt fantastic.

'It was south London's Barbary Coast,' Paul remembers with a smile. And he was desperate to be part of it. His first job in SE1 was at the Elephant & Castle pub – somewhere he could walk to from his council flat on the South Lambeth Road and where he knew most of his friends would be propping up the other side of the bar. Happy to share a laugh with his mates while flirting outrageously, if unsuccessfully, with the punters, Paul felt at home from his first shift. It wasn't exactly a classy joint – but then neither were the brothels he had loved in all those westerns he had watched as a kid.

The most jaw-dropping night of the week was the not-entirely accurately named Ladies' Night. Anyone and everyone was invited to climb up on to the tiny, triangular stage to show their party piece. Paul remembers strippers who would go as far as taking their false teeth out, people who would lie down on broken glass without knowing how to do it, comedians who hadn't realised the audience should be laughing with not at them. But what Paul and the other punters remember the most is the ragbag of blokes who were too tall, too burly and too hairy – but who still wanted to bob around and pretend they were Barbra Streisand.

'I'd think, Oh Christ, another lorry driver who fancies himself as Liza Minnelli. They all wore the sequins and feather boas and spoke falsetto, and it could be painful to watch,' Paul says. Interestingly, Paul never once considered taking a few minutes out from behind the bar to get on to the stage himself. He was having fun creating his characters at home with Alan and Brendan. But he couldn't see his idea of Lily lip-synching to the latest disco diva's hit.

Two things changed all that. First was the news that the regular compère for the Ladies' Night wasn't going to able to do the show the following week. Second came the revelation that he was paid £15 more than the bar staff for the same length shift.

'I'll do it,' said Paul, volunteering himself for the role before he had time to think about it.

'You'd better be good,' was all the manager said to him, as his name went on the bill.

Paul walked home in a state of shock. He wasn't exactly sure what he had let himself in for. But he knew he had less than a week to bring Lily Savage to life. Getting a costume together was his first big challenge, and Paul was determined not to fall into any of the traps he had seen at the Elephant & Castle to date.

'I got an old coat from a market and a handbag. I knew I wasn't going to be Shirley Bassey,' Paul says. But the trip to the market did more than give Paul the first bit of kit he needed for Lily. It also reminded him of a day years earlier at a similar market in Sheffield. Back then he had seen a woman laden with shopping, with two children next to her in a battered buggy, giving a stall holder a mouthful about something she had bought the week before. Paul had stopped in his tracks to watch and to listen. He couldn't take his eyes off her.

'Most people would have been repelled by her. She was wearing this lairy outfit and white stilettos. She had a peroxide-white beehive, heavy make-up, and a charm bracelet and earrings that were probably in and out of the pawnbrokers. The kids were vile, all snot and ice cream. But I took a shine to her.'

And he didn't forget her. Memories of that anonymous woman on the Sheffield market would help him frame Lily down in London. And so many other women from

Paul's past would also get conjured up as he prepared his act in that first nervous week.

'When I caught a glimpse of myself in the mirror as Lily, I saw my mother or my auntie. It's familiar; so many women of the family come through. Lily is mothers, aunties, neighbours, the slightly racy women who lived up the road.' Lily might seem like a hideous caricature to some of her audiences. But to Paul she would never be anything but real.

Just how the catcalling, heckling regulars at the Elephant & Castle's Ladies' Night would treat her was another matter. And just before his first-ever performance Paul was far more nervous than he had expected. He was sitting sweating and feeling sick in the pub's tiny, harshly lit dressing room with Brendan and two other friends as the bar filled up. 'Why aren't I just pulling pints like normal?' he kept wailing. 'Why couldn't I have been happy as Bet Lynch? Do I really need all this heartache for fifteen bleeding pounds?'

And for all the jokes and the bravado Brendan and the others could tell that Paul was genuinely terrified. He was stepping so far out of his comfort zone – while wearing deliberately scuffed white stilettos. It didn't promise to be an easy journey and when he was finally pushed on to the stage Paul admits he nearly blew it.

The usual mixed bag of strippers, jokers and drag artists were lined up waiting for their moment in the spotlight. But Paul almost forgot to introduce them. 'My nerves were so shot that I rabbited on for about an hour before I introduced the first act,' he says. But amazingly enough, when Paul did call up the first performer, the audience actually started to boo. They wanted more of Paul – or at least of Lily. Despite his crippling nerves, Paul's hour-long rant had been comic gold. It was roughly hewn and in need of polish. But it was gold all the same.

Never one to show off about his talents, Paul does admit that something had gone very right when he picked up the microphone that night in 1985. 'All those years of messing around and play-acting with my mates at home just came out. I didn't have an act as such. I just talked. I was going on about fiddling the electricity meter and signing on late. I talked about drugs and shoplifting and sex, all the things you weren't supposed to mention back then. I knew all about it because if I hadn't done it I had certainly seen it. And I knew instinctively how Lily would be, how she would walk and smoke and how she would think.'

When the punters yelled out a few times he was ready, as Lily, to throw some insult right back at them. When he lost his train of thought on one anecdote, he just picked straight up with another. That smoky, croaky Scouse voice hit every corner of the bar and got every drinker paying attention. The sneers, the asides and the arch glances at the audience when the acts were finally given a chance to do their stuff were equally right. Lily Savage was alive – and everyone wanted her back again the following week.

For that second performance the crowd wouldn't have been happy with anything less than an hour-long introduction to the acts. In fact, the first act Lily brought into the lights was booed – because, once again, the punters didn't want Lily to leave the stage.

Comedy experts who saw some of those early performances and have tracked Paul's career ever since say that what worked was the fact that Paul got the details right with Lily. His creation was someone he really did know, who lived a life he could describe with total accuracy. The crisis loans, the Mighty White bread, the nightmare of feeding a cat when you've got a hangover – everything rang true. While middle-class comedians might base sketches around their characters going up in front of a judge, Paul knew that someone like Lily was far more likely to be up in front of a magistrate. It was a small but telling difference.

'Paul inhabited Lily Savage from the very start and that showed itself in a host of different ways,' says fellow stand-up Lloyd Pierce. 'What it also did was give him the confidence to really go for it. Nothing succeeds like success and nothing stinks like failure. But when Paul was on form as Lily he was succeeding so much that he could tell he had the audience in the palm of his hand. That in turn allowed him to let rip and take her anywhere he wanted to go. What you need as a stand-up is to be in perfect harmony with your alter ego. Right from the start you couldn't get a cigarette paper between Paul and Lily. That's why she did so well.'

For his part, Paul admits that the audience reaction blew him away. He simply couldn't believe how well everyone responded to Lily – and being on stage as her was like a bizarre out-of-body experience. Everything was coming out of his head, but he knew he could only say the words when he was in her clothes. It was an extraordinarily liberating experience. 'If I didn't have Lily and went on stage as myself I would be worried about what I was saying because it would be my opinions. With Lily it's just a raving lunatic's perspective on life. An old cow ranting about a spin dryer falling from the twenty-fourth floor and hitting her on the head. It's fantasy but it's wonderful.'

Brendan Murphy saw things exactly the same way. By putting on such an extreme persona he knew Paul could say and do the things everyone else only dreamed about. 'You and I would never say what we think to the milkman, for example, but Lily would, without even paying lip service to convention. It's like in the movies when characters take out their frustrations by driving cars through a showroom window. It's a nice idea, but who would ever do it in real life?'

The wild abandon of Lily's early act was sending shockwaves through the club scene for other reasons too. Paul felt no connection to the female impersonators of yesteryear and had no reason to stick to the conventions of the genre. 'Drag acts in the past, like Dame Edna and Hinge and Brackett, have all been matrons – sexless and with no chests. Danny La Rue was very glamorous but, again, he was sexless. Lily, though, was always going to be predatory. Short skirts, leopard skin, red talons and loads of make-up.'

Time Out reporter Paul Kinleigh remembers some of Lily's first few appearances and says the divide between past and present was impossible to miss. 'Yes, there was a lot of coarse humour on the drag scene back then, but the very few long-established acts who had made it out of the gay pubs and into the mainstream still seemed to be based around some idealised portrait of the ideal, effortlessly glamorous woman. Danny La Rue was basically the Duchess of Kent. Lily Savage didn't even come close to the Duchess of Duke Street. The old crowd were impersonating perfect women who didn't really exist. Paul was impersonating someone so awful we didn't want her to exist.'

Paul's only objection to comments like this was the fact that he never saw himself as impersonating women. All he was ever doing was putting on a show – it just happened that the show was based around a woman called Lily. 'You'd have to be Helen Keller not to know I was a bloke and I'm not cross-dressing, I'm cross-dressing-down,' he would say.

He was also wary of comparisons with other performers from the gay scene who had hit the mainstream. In 1985, he was hardly in the same league. A few weekly shows in the corner of a south London pub hardly constituted a whole new career – especially when all he got at the end of the night was a sore throat and a thin envelope containing just four ten pound notes. Being Lily Savage back then was still just a bit of fun. Or it was until someone spoke to Paul at the end of one of his Elephant & Castle gigs.

It was the manager from the Royal Vauxhall Tavern, a much bigger gay bar just around the corner. Word of mouth said Lily was going to be a big draw on the pub scene, so the Vauxhall Tavern wanted to sign her up as soon as possible. Hardly able to believe he was being poached, Paul agreed to jump ships. Maybe Lily Savage might turn into something more than just a bit of fun? Maybe she might take him somewhere? Still desperate not to tempt fate, even Paul couldn't stop himself from dreaming just a little bit about where his comic creation might end up. They were exciting times indeed for Paul, Brendan and his increasingly close group of pals.

At the Royal Vauxhall Tavern, Lily's job was to start off with a topical, rambling introduction and then introduce the 'stars of the future' on what the pub called the 'illuminated runway of joy'. Lily was also there to provide a running commentary on them – often the highlight of the night. It was Simon Cowell, a generation before his time. The night was called Duckie and under Paul's influence it would become an extraordinary blend of talent show and old-fashioned music hall entertainment. Lily would perform there every week for almost eight long years.

Along the way Paul, Brendan, their old friend Alan

and several others in Paul's inner circle would all help hone and refine the act. As usual, Paul was always looking at women in the streets, on buses, in supermarkets and pubs. He was picking up tiny extra details to take on to his stage. The aim was to produce an air of glamour gone ever so slightly sour. Dark roots would often show through one of Lily's platinum blond wigs. Holes would appear in her tights and after buying brand new white stilettos for the act, Paul would make sure they were scuffed and worn by the time they appeared on stage. Lily, he vowed, would be the blonde bombsite, the ultimate Liver Bird on the make.

And he loved Dolly Parton's old line that it costs a fortune to look so cheap. The kind of sequined ocelot-print fabric he knew would be perfect for Lily's costumes (which he was starting to have made up especially for him) cost around £90 a metre. Two friends, one a tailor and the other a hairdresser, joined forces to perfect the look for as low a price as possible. When Paul wasn't worrying about what he should wear on stage he was busy working on what he should say. At first he decided to deliberately insult whole sections of his audiences before they could attack him – being offensive is the best form of defence, he used to say. But after a while he realised he didn't actually have any problems when the hecklers tried to stop him mid-flow. The banter and the backchat got his adrenaline flowing, and out of nowhere he always seemed able to find the perfect put-down, the ultimate insult. And he was throwing his poisoned barbs from a position of strength. He was nearly six foot two even before he pulled on Lily's high heels and climbed on to the stage. He didn't have much trouble dominating the crowd.

Paul's love of a good story also came to his rescue in Lily's early days. All the tales his aunts, uncles and neighbours had spun in Birkenhead and in Ireland would inspire him to weave an intricate background story for his new creation. And so, he declared, Lilian May Veronica Savage was the offspring of a Birkenhead wrestler called Hellcat Savage and a passing Irish seaman – Lily knows he was Irish because she says her mother remembers a rugged Irish accent saying: 'How much?' as he walked away. As a child Lily had her hair dyed before she even hit school: 'The peroxide and the toothbrush came out at three years old. "I'm not having a ginger-haired baby, get on that dye," my mother told me,' Lily would say to her appalled audiences.

Of her later life, Paul decided that Lily would be wildly proud of being named Miss New Brighton Baths in her youth, though she would remain evasive over exactly how long ago the title had been won. Her legitimate career peaked when she was made senior counter assistant on the pic'n'mix in the Lambeth Woolworths. But her real work was done in the black economy, a world Paul knew only too well.

'Didn't you used to be a social worker?' was one of the favourite questions Paul got his mates to ask during the question-and-answer part of some of his early shows.

'Yes I did. Well, at least that's what I told the magistrates. They still gave me three months, though,' Paul fired back, quick as a shot. 'But I did help old men. Though not exactly to get across the road.'

It was a clever mix of his own experiences at work and his own unique imagination. For the more recent part of Lily's life, Paul billed her as an international sex kitten – supposedly mingling with jet-setters and celebrities alike. But he said she wasn't exactly over the moon when Sir David Attenborough supposedly mistook her blond beehive for a Maori hut.

Lily's personal life remained just as vivid. Her position in the League of Catholic Mothers would never be entirely secure, though Paul happily created Lily's own happy family. There was her grandmother, Erica von Savage who died of hypothermia after shoplifting frozen turkeys from Bejam. Then there was daughter Bunty, who dumped her daughter Kylie Marie on Lily when she got bored with her. Also in the story was her son Jason (the Stockwell Arsonist) who spent most of his time in Risley remand centre. Her sister Vera and whippet Queenie (both then incontinent) were equal favourites among the south London crowds. Fans said there was something in the way Lily delivered her lines that meant they could be heard several times without losing their laughs. And a lot of the humour was relatively gentle.

'Oh, I remember those family holidays at that seaside when Vera went behind a rock to look for crabs. "Come

back, Vera, you haven't got them," I would yell at her,'
Lily rasped. Then there were the long, hilarious and
archly described stories of Vera's ill-fated marriage.
'Something happened on the wedding night. Vera never
spoke about it again. All we knew was the twenty-two
piece dinner service off the Embassy coupons was
smashed in a fit of pique in the bedroom.'

To add to the fun Paul decided to make his Lily a
hypochondriac, a drama queen and a dreamer. He had
her go to Lourdes, even though all she had was a verruca.
He had her in constant trouble with the law. And he
made sure she was always keeping herself one step ahead
of the game. 'This is Zandra Rhodes, this outfit. She
doesn't know I've got it, but I do her service washes,' Lily
boasted, between endless drags on her cigarettes.

Regulars from the south London pubs in the mid- to
late-1980s also remember hearing many of Lily's best
lines long before they were aired on television.

'The best one was the one about her smoking at the
airport,' says Paul Kinleigh.

'I was having a crafty ciggie there the other day and
this cleaner pointed to the non-smoking sign and said:
"Can't you read?" I said: "Yes I can, that's why I'm not
washing floors in a bleedin' airport." Cheeky bitch.'

Lily's plays on words were also part of the fun. 'I'm in
an open marriage,' Lily would say, languidly. 'I'm 'open
he's going to piss off with someone else.' All the while,
what kept the act ringing true was the way Lily acted,
the way she walked, the way she stood, the way she

prowled around the still tiny patch of stage. Reaching inside her bra to pull out a packet of cigarettes could bring the house down however often she did it. Cursing at her soundmen or the guys in charge of her backing music did the same.

She was, quite literally, as far from the traditional drag tradition as a pair of scuffed-up stilettos can take you. And she wasn't entirely alone. At that time, a growing band of tougher new acts were spicing up the drag, comedy and club scene. One of Paul's pals – and one of his rivals – was Reginald Bundy. He was nine years older and appeared as the incomparable Her Imperial Highness Regina Fong. With a flame-red wig and a matching ball gown, Regina was also busy working on a background story to die for. Regina, Reg decided, was a member of the Romanoff family who escaped the storming of the Winter Palace in St Petersburg in 1917 and ended up living in Berkshire 'under the protection of the British royal family'. Just like Paul, Reg would incorporate topical references and contemporary culture into his act and didn't take any prisoners when his audiences decided to play up.

Other mouthy big acts of the day (or more accurately the night) were being created by the likes of Dave Lynn, Paul Searle, Roy Powell and Paul Banks. Everyone knew everyone else and everyone was competing to get the first really big break. So the atmosphere backstage wasn't always very friendly.

Meanwhile, at the Royal Vauxhall Tavern Paul was

finally earning a good bit more than his original £40 pay packet – Brendan had taken on an informal role as his tough-talking manager to try and make the act seem like a bigger and more professional concern. But for all the fun, the laughs and the money it was still an exhausting business. Paul would arrive at the pub after yet another long day's work with the council. And he would arrive long before show time – because in those early days it still took him a good two hours to get ready for every performance. Slowly learning some tricks of the drag trade opened up some short cuts. But being Lily was never for the faint-hearted.

The transformation began with Paul climbing into what he described as the kind of harness that the NHS puts you in if you break your back in a car accident. One of his favourites was made of whalebone, worked like a corset, and made his eyes water when it was tightened around his waist. His reinforced bras were hollow – when he was in a big enough venue to need one, he put his radio mike in the left cup, his fags and lighter in the right. He refused to pluck his eyebrows, so he used mortician's wax to blot them out when he made up his face. And no matter how revealing his costume, he also refused to shave his chest, legs or anywhere else. Instead he would pull on two pairs of dancers' tights then a final pair of ordinary tights to give his long thin legs what would soon be their famous sheen. The wig, which could add an extra foot and a half to his height and a surprisingly large amount to his weight, was normally the last part of his costume to go on, not least because it was so hot to wear. His own already greying hair was held back in a tight net underneath and the wig was attached with more than half a dozen pins.

'When all that's done I feel like I've sold my soul. Paul has gone. He has been swapped for a harpy called Lily,' Paul would say. And as his act developed, the harpy was starting to play in some pretty special halls. He worked briefly at the famous Madame JoJo's club in London's Soho where fellow comedian Mark Thomas remembers how much his co-star enjoyed teasing the audiences. 'Blokes in the crowd would send messages backstage asking Lily to come and join them for champagne. So after the show Paul would change out of his togs and appear without make-up or wig, just in jeans and T-shirt and say: "Thanks very much, mate." These guys would be flabbergasted. I don't know what it was they expected, but it wasn't what they got.'

Paul also suffered indignities as his act went out on the road. The pub circuit was still a low-rent, hard knocks world and the dressing rooms in many of his venues were simply corridors or staff toilets. Many was the time that punters burst in on the transformation process – one night someone grabbed Paul's wig and ran back out into the bar with it. Shocked drinkers remember that a fight nearly broke out before the wig was forcibly returned to its owner and Paul could finally take to the stage. Then there was the night when the police raided the Royal Vauxhall Tavern. Paul, horrified at the thought that this was some sort of attack on the gay community, was in no mood to co-operate with the authorities, even when he was carted off in full costume to Brixton police station.

'Name?' he remembers the desk sergeant asking.

'Lily Savage,' he replied, refusing to give an inch.

'Real name.'

'Lilian Veronica May Savage.'

But for all the uncertainties of life on the bottom rung of the entertainment ladder, Paul was thriving in his new environment. He was still working for Camden Council every day. But he was dreaming about showbusiness every night. Being Lily Savage had started to earn him a decent extra income but he was ready to ditch her if more mainstream entertainment work came his way. Paul, the late starter, suddenly had an urge to perform anywhere and for anyone. So he started to quiz his friends and fellow drinkers for any tips on how to break into the arts industry full-time. He considered acting classes, tried to get into Equity and went on the audition trail for a series of commercials and advertising campaigns.

Unfortunately for him, one of his earliest breaks would end in a typically surreal disaster. It was late 1986 and Paul had won the lead in a south London production of *What Ever Happened to Baby Jane?* It wasn't south London as in the National Theatre, or the Old Vic, Paul is happy to point out. More south London as in a pub theatre just off Kennington Lane where the camp classic had a ready-made audience. Halfway through one Saturday night performance, Paul caught his knee in the wheelchair he had to perform in, and felt the bone snap out of its socket. He was taken to King's College Hospital – still dressed as Baby Jane. With casualty full of drunks and accident victims Paul was left to fend for himself for nearly four hours – at which point he ran out of patience and made the mistake of trying to crack some jokes to get noticed.

'Don't you remember me? I'm Baby Jane Hudson,' he shouted when a doctor finally came to check him out. 'Next time I woke up I was in the psychiatric ward with this guy in the bed opposite throwing his dinner at me,' he remembers with a laugh. It took an urgent call for a friend to come over and assure the doctors that Paul wasn't as mad as he looked before he got discharged.

Until the end of the 1980s Paul slogged away on the cabaret circuit, his long days at work followed by late nights on the boards. The good news was that his act was starting to break free of the south London gay ghetto and he was being booked into lengthy tours of venues all across the country and beyond. When he thought it would help, he joined forces with several of the other pub and club performers in a series of double and triple acts – High Society, The Playgirls and The Glamazons being the most successful. He took to the stage everywhere from Denmark and Finland to France, Germany and even Israel and made his first single, riding the hi-NRG disco wave with 'Tough at the Top' produced by the music mogul and DJ Ian Levine. 'I'm climbing my way up the ladder,' Lily spat out in the song, just as Paul was trying to do in real life.

But for Paul, climbing up the ladder meant that he was always working, always on the road. Sometimes he felt as if his whole holiday allowance was taken up travelling around with Lily's costumes and wigs in a bin liner. But what could he do? Deep down he knew he had to decide between his full-time career and his ongoing love of performing. But the desire for financial stability that had been drummed into him since childhood made him wary of making the leap. He had the job with the pension that his parents had always wanted for him. Could he really give it up for something as fickle as showbusiness?

Towards the end of 1988 Paul finally got the push to do just that. He was approached by the producers of *The Bill* – the police show that had just been launched on ITV and would turn out to be one of the channel's biggest long-term hits. They wanted Paul to play the part of a cross-dressing informer called Roxanne in an early episode called *No Strings*. It would be a huge piece of national exposure for Paul – who had decided to sign up under his then stage name of Paul Savage.

So after spending weeks doing sums in his head and working out how long he could survive if his income dried up, Paul gave his letter of resignation to his head of department at Camden Council. His new life of adventure was about to begin. 'I'm on my way,' he told himself, as he went out to celebrate with his mates. But what he didn't know was that an enormous blow was about to push him off course. Once more, tragedy was going to strike in Birkenhead and again Paul would discover that good things always seemed to carry a terrible price.

CHAPTER FOUR

Tragedy

In the first few months of 1989, no one knew if *The Bill* would capture the public imagination and be a hit. It was filmed in Wapping, east London, and crew members say there was a fantastic atmosphere on set with plenty of laughs and deep friendships formed. Paul was in his element and was thriving on the atmosphere of a major big budget new show. He knew his character was hardly going to be central to the series. But in showbusiness you never knew where even the smallest break might lead. And already Lily seemed to be in demand. It looked as if success really could breed success.

After his first scenes were shot in east London Paul headed up to Nottingham where Lily had won herself a mini-tour of the city's clubs. Night after night, club after club Paul strode across the stage firing out his anecdotes, lashing back at the punters and having the time of his life. Or at least he was until he came back home to London in the early hours of the morning after one late-night gig. Walking into his flat, the first thing he saw was the light flashing furiously on his answering machine. For some reason he knew instinctively that this could only mean bad news.

'Paul, give us a ring.' The first message was from his sister and as soon as he heard it Paul's blood froze. Immediately, he says, he knew exactly why she was calling.

'Paul, you'd better ring quickly.' The second message served only to confirm his fears. And he hardly needed to listen to all the others. His own tears began to fall as soon as he heard the sound of others' tears on the next messages. His mother had died, probably at the exact same time that he had taken to the stage that night in Nottingham. It was, he says, as if his entire life was being played out on an answering machine tape.

Within hours Paul was on the first train up to Liverpool that he could find, sitting in silence all the way north, thinking back to all the highs and lows of his extraordinary childhood. He thought of the sacrifices his mother had made to raise her family. He thought of her wit and her passion. Of her sharp tongue, her dry humour, her endless, unconditional love. He also realised that she would never now get to see her son appear on television. So she would never really know about this extraordinary new chapter in his life.

Molly and the rest of the family in Birkenhead all knew that Paul had an act which he took around the pubs and clubs of London and beyond. But his mother in particular had never seen him on stage as Lily Savage. Paul had always been hugely protective of his mother – and indeed of his late father. So he hadn't ever wanted them to face up to issues or circumstances they might not understand. 'As far as my mum was concerned I kept quiet about Lily. I just didn't want to tell my family I went around the clubs dressed as some old tart. My prejudice, not hers,' he says quietly, his words drawing a line under the subject as one he doesn't want to return to.

It was the same with his sexuality. The rest of his family might have talked about 'Paul's madness' but his mother had never really spoken of it. And now that she had gone, Paul refused to apologise for keeping the subject buried himself. 'There were things I never discussed with her but that was right. My whole aim in life was not to get my mum worried. I tried to protect her. I wasn't lying. I just kept my mouth shut. I didn't want to think of her at home in bed worrying what I was up to. It was a case of what the eye doesn't see, and all that.'

It had been the same more than a decade earlier when his father had still been alive. Paul had long since wanted to tell his dad that he thought he might be gay. But he had never been able to find the right time. 'I used to see him playing the squeeze box and think: "How can I tell him? I won't. I don't want to ruin his day." I kept a lot from both of them because I didn't want to upset them.'

Back in London after his mother's funeral, an exhausted and still depressed Paul began to re-evaluate his life. Time suddenly seemed shorter, fate more mercurial. He had seen yet again that the good times could quite literally come and go in a heartbeat. So he felt he had to carry on grasping life with both hands, to squeeze as much as possible out of every single day. He vowed to accept the very next job he was offered. And as luck would have it this would in itself change his life once more. The job didn't pay him much money and didn't push on his career in any major way. But it would ultimately produce a far more valuable result. Paul was about to make a lifelong friend just when he needed one the most.

'I hate these things.'

'I hate them too.'

Paul looked over at the woman who had just sat next to him in the cold north London rehearsal room. The room was full of actors who were all busily gossiping about their latest triumphs at the Royal Court theatre on Sloane Square. No one wanted to talk to him, which was just as well as he didn't think they would be very impressed hearing about his latest stand-up gig at the Royal Oak pub in the East End. So as the room filled up, the chair next to him was the only one to remain empty

– until this beautiful, bored-looking woman in a leather biker's jacket threw herself into it.

Her name, Paul would soon find out, was Amanda Mealing – then fresh from *Grange Hill*, soon to be even more famous as Connie Beauchamp in *Holby City*. 'She sat down, lit up and took a long drag on her cigarette, like Bette Davis. It took her so long to exhale. She had a real whiff of trouble about her and that's what attracted me to her,' Paul remembers of the woman some twelve years his junior.

The strange attraction was mutual. 'I don't know what it was about him, but we just bonded, we fitted together like a nice jigsaw puzzle,' says Amanda. 'We weren't jaded about things but I think we both had this slightly jaded approach. We had both been around for so long that the novelty of what we do had worn off. I had been working since I was six and Paul is an old-fashioned vaudeville act, born out of time. So treading the boards was in our blood. And we both liked to laugh about it.'

The pair were in the rehearsal room with three dozen other actors to prepare for a very special set of performances at the King's Head theatre just up the road in Islington. It was called *Elegies for Angels, Punks and Raging Queens* – though after looking around the room at their new colleagues, Paul and Amanda soon agreed that Ageing Queens might be a more accurate description of the cast. Despite the typical gallows humour the show itself was intensely moving. The whole cast each performed a two-minute monologue about a friend or lover who had died of Aids coming back to them. Those were the days when Aids still seemed an absolute death sentence and Paul and Amanda already had too many friends in mind when they spoke their lines.

Backstage at the King's Head was controlled chaos. The thirty key players had to get changed and made-up wherever there was space – Paul and Amanda chose an office, which meant they had to scramble over some scaffolding and down a ladder to get to the stage. They were only on in the second act and the finale, so they had plenty of time to chat and to get to know each other. And perhaps in order to take their minds off the grim subject of the evenings, they always tried to keep things light – perhaps too light. Having realised they shared almost identical senses of humour, they knew they could never risk meeting each other's eye on stage, especially during the final song. 'One look at Savage and I'd have blown it,' says Amanda.

The show lasted for six weeks with everyone involved pretty much giving their time for free. The cast was just paid 'expenses' of £5 a week. And Paul and Amanda spent it fast. 'A whole bunch of the cast would go out, but somehow at four in the morning there would only be me and Savage stumbling out of some Soho club,' Amanda remembers. Fortunately, she had a flat on Shaftsbury Avenue and Paul would crash there on a near-nightly basis. It was a favour he was pleased to return some two decades later when Amanda had moved to the country and was able to stay at Paul's Tower Bridge home when she was in town filming *Holby City* over at the Elstree studios.

With his charitable work out of the way and a new friend in his gang, Paul was ready for his next serious career challenge in 1989. For the past few years he, Brendan and a group of their other pals had been regular visitors to the Edinburgh Festival. It felt like a huge, endless party where the booze flowed freely and the company was electric. But everyone knew that there was a serious side to the visits as well. Both the fringe and the main stages offered fantastic showcases for up and coming comedy acts. In the late 1980s, Paul and the gang had watched the likes of Jeremy Hardy, Simon Fanshawe and Sean Hughes make huge breakthroughs in the middle of the chaos and confusion of the festival. So could Lily Savage win the same kind of break for Paul?

For a long time it didn't seem likely because Paul realised there were a lot of bridges to cross and a lot of attitudes to change before a drag act could win over the Edinburgh intelligentsia. 'In the first years in Edinburgh I could sense it. I could sense the other performers who looked at me as if to say: "My God, what's the Festival coming to?" I was made to feel as if I shouldn't be there,' he said.

But the fighter in Paul wasn't to be put off so easily. He brought Lily back to Scotland the following year – and the year after that. By 1991, he had finally got the audiences, the critics and the comedy judges paying attention. That year Paul found himself alongside Jack Dee, Eddie Izzard and Frank Skinner in the running for the flagship Perrier Award – the prize long since known as the Oscar of comedy. Frank Skinner was the eventual winner, but Paul's nomination triggered huge celebrations among his inner circle of friends. Heading back to London, he and Brendan were exhausted but ecstatic. And they were about to get some extraordinarily good news.

Lily's appeal had by now extended far beyond the south London gay scene. Even the mainstream comedy clubs were starting to feel a little too small for the act. So a team of producers had decided she should do her first major theatre show. And they wanted it filmed for posterity. *Lily Savage Live from the Hackney Empire* was to be the biggest professional event of Paul's life.

The theatre had a capacity of more than 1,200 people – and by the time the big night came around, every seat had been sold. Walking down Mare Street for the first of his rehearsals Paul says he felt an incredible buzz – because no theatre seemed to suit him as well as the Hackney Empire. Built in 1901, it had been the technological wonder of its age, promising electric lights, central heating and a specially made projection box for the stage. Charlie Chaplin had been one of its early performers and Stan Laurel had made some of his first appearances on its stage. In the 1920s and 30s, the theatre was also the UK home of burlesque, the classic, risqué theatre that Paul had always adored. And in the post-war years the Empire would play host for everyone from Tony Hancock to Liberace. Paul vowed that Lily Savage would strut on to its stage as if she owned it. This was her showbusiness heritage, after all. She would revel in every minute.

Having the show filmed was another brilliant first for Paul. Playing to cameras as well as to more than a thousand paying punters was a challenge. But having a record of an entire show would be a superb calling card for future work. It would make Paul a bit of extra money. And he could re-watch it endlessly as he perfected his act for the future.

In the meantime, Paul wasn't taking any chances. He was still terrified that the work could dry up at any time so he continued to audition for as many diverse roles as possible. After the Hackney Empire gig, Paul's acting alter ego, Paul Savage, won a role in a four-part ITV drama called *Chimera*. The show, about an improbable half-man, half-ape on the loose in Cumbria, involved some long days on location, required Paul to learn rudimentary sign-language and once more helped him make a firm new friend. This time it was a still-unknown actress and comedian called Liza Tarbuck, who would work with him many times in the years ahead. Shortly after leaving the set of *Chimera*, Paul won a brighter role playing Marlene Dietrich in the Rik Mayall show *The New Statesman*.

Those were frenetic, stressful times. But however

many other roles Paul signed up for, it seemed as if Lily was the one the audiences wanted to see the most. He spent almost all of the next six months on the road as a 'Perrier Award-nominated' star – and one who could flog videos in the theatre foyers to supplement his income still further. Back in Edinburgh the following summer he was finally feeling comfortable about his act. In 1992 you tried to look down on Lily Savage at your peril. That said, not everything went smoothly at Festival time. Up in Scotland and living it large, Paul was about to suffer his first tabloid mauling.

It happened late one night when Paul was celebrating a successful performance with a group of theatre colleagues and reporters. They were squeezed into his favourite bar in the capital – CC Bloom's, named after Bette Midler's character in the film *Beaches*. Someone in the crowd handed Paul a giant fake joint as a joke, while someone else took a picture. It felt like another harmless night out and Paul certainly didn't think he was famous enough to worry about any repercussions. But two days later the photograph was all over the Scottish *Daily Record* under the headline: LILY LIKES A JOINT.

'I was well and truly set up,' he says, though he was secretly thrilled to be deemed so important. Other reporters were also crowding around him after his shows, desperate to get the inside scoop on the man who had become one of the surprise hits of the Festival. But Paul says he wasn't always very good at answering them. 'The worst was the journalist from one of the

Top: Louder than Lily? Surely not! Ms Savage in 1993

Bottom: Lily at the 1994 Albert Hall evening organised by Stonewall with Elton John and Sting.

Top: In bed with Lily in 1995, who took over from Paula Yates on *The Big Breakfast*.

Bottom left: Playing in the stage version of *Prisoner Cell Block H* with Maggie Kirkpatrick in 1995.

Bottom right: Gayle Tuesday, page 3 stunna – also known as Paul's friend Brenda Gilhooly.

Paul with daughter Sharyn in 1995.

Paul in 1996.

Lily at the BAFTA Awards in 1998

Top: Relaxing at home with furry friends.

Bottom: In town and more evil than ever – the wicked queen in panto in Bristol, 2003.

Paul with his friend Barbara Windsor...

...and with another friend, Cilla Black

broadsheets who asked lots of deep questions about my motivation and where the initial ideas for Lily had come from. I felt obliged to say that I'd done loads of workshops and research with the character. When of course I'd done no real research whatsoever. I'd just kept my eyes open all my life. After all, Lily was just me with a wig on acting daft.'

For someone whose act had such a strong visual appeal it was ironic that Paul's next big breakthrough would come on radio. And for an act that was so close to the bone and steeped in such bad language it was equally strange that the first radio station to take him to its heart was Radio 4. But Lily became a regular guest on shows like *Woman's Hour* and *Loose Ends*, as well as talking on *Vibe* on the new Radio Five Live.

'What do you want for Christmas, Lily?'

'Anything with a receipt.'

Paul was constantly updating and refining Lily's act with lines like these throughout the early 1990s – he loved having to think on his feet and answer questions from the radio presenters and the crowds. And his responses were getting him noticed. Ever since his breakthrough in Edinburgh, Paul and Brendan's phones had finally started to ring, as agents, bookers and casting directors tried to sign up the act. It was a fantastic relief for both men not to have to be the ones to be constantly pushing the act themselves, cold-calling people to try and book gigs for Lily. But for all this new-found success, both men knew it was far too early to relax. They were well aware that even the hottest stars can go cold overnight – and both felt that Lily still had a long way to go.

'For someone like Paul, the crucial thing when you're on the cusp of fame is to do anything and everything,' says Sasha Browning, the casting agent who would eventually get Paul one of his first spots on Channel 4. 'Television is a ridiculously strange medium. Hundreds of people are working for practically nothing because they are so desperate to get on to a show, while a tiny number are effectively saying they won't get out of bed for less than a telephone number pay cheque. Everyone knows you can go from zero to hero almost overnight if you've got the talent and you find yourself in the right place at the right time. I knew that Paul had the talent and it was obvious that he was finally starting to catch the right people's eyes.'

After Sasha put in some calls Paul did get a spot on Channel 4 – on the late-night comedy and music showcase *Viva Cabaret!* Competition for a slot on the first series of 50-minute shows was intense because almost every rising star of the comedy circuit was trying to get on board. Alongside Paul were the likes of Mark Thomas, Harry Hill, Julian Clary, Rowland Rivron and Greg Proops.

Once more, Paul was to make a good friend on the show; this time, Brenda Gilhooly, whose 'page three stunna' Gayle Tuesday would soon be joining Lily on tour. Up in Birkenhead there were plenty of open mouths at 10.30pm when the first show aired. Though Paul had been working in the clubs for nearly a decade, very few of his family or neighbours had seen the act before. But everyone loved it.

'I was amazed and he was fantastic,' sister Shelagh says of that debut, one of the first of the few times she had ever seen her brother dressed as a woman. Interestingly enough, she immediately spotted the similarities to so many of the people who had wandered through the O'Grady house in their childhood. 'Paul was obviously developing the character of Lily Savage all along,' she said, ticking off all the aunts and neighbours that she recognised in his act.

Shelagh and the neighbours all said Paul was the true star of *Viva Cabaret!*, overshadowing even the big name guests like Tom Jones and Eartha Kitt. The Merseysiders turned out to be right. Paul and Brendan soon got a call from the BBC and it looked as if Lily might finally be about to go mainstream. She had been asked to appear on her first TV quiz show, the BBC's *That's Showbusiness*. It wasn't exactly cutting edge stuff (one critic called it, 'So middle-of-the-road it hurts') but it had the possibility to be a wonderful platform from which to shine. As long as Lily stayed on her best behaviour. Paul knew a few pantomime-style double entendres might be acceptable, but swearing and dodgy adult humour was out. The show's style was frothy, fun and frivolous.

But for Paul his first appearance was pretty much a disaster. The show was filmed in studios in Manchester and he managed to leave Lily's costume and her wig on the train. So instead of providing a huge showcase for Lily Savage, he had to go on camera as himself – a hugely stressful occasion and one he swore he would never repeat.

Fortunately, for his second appearance he had Lily's armour to hide behind and so he sparkled. Lily was on top form and in her element. Fans said she made a huge impact among the other better-known celebrity guests. And all the mainstream mums and dads watching at home laughed like drains at her arch asides and flat Scouse growls.

But while *That's Showbusiness* meant a whole new set of commissioning editors, producers and directors started to take notice, Lily failed to get as many call-backs as Paul and Brendan had hoped. The idea had been that as soon as Lily went on prime time television her phone would be red hot. But it wasn't turning out to be quite so easy. Interestingly, Paul says it wasn't specifically because he was a man in drag. The real problem, he felt, was that he was a man playing a woman.

'Because of Lily I am treated as a woman and TV is much more wary of female comics, be they Jo Brand or Gayle Tuesday, or whoever. However, if you're a bloke in a T-shirt and jeans, you do a couple of nights at Jongleurs and you're almost guaranteed your own series. Go on stage as a boring old bloke and moan about the state of the world and you'll be on BBC2 before you get back to your changing room. Go on stage as a woman and television just doesn't know what to do with you.'

So while he waited for the industry to work it out Paul decided to get on a plane. He had won an acting job in his beloved Dublin – and he fancied a chance to catch up with some old friends. His role was as a prisoner in the big-budget Daniel Day-Lewis film *In the Name of the Father*. Paul moved in with fellow drag star Alan Amsby for the duration of the shoot. They had a ball. 'We painted the town red every night,' says Alan, whose drag act headlined at Mr Pussy's Café on Suffolk Street – where everyone from Bono to the writer and director Jim Sheridan would hang out. But Alan remembers that it wasn't all partying with Paul that year. He and his old friend also had plenty of long heart-to-heart talks about their futures, with Paul proving to be far more serious and sensible than many people might have expected. Alan, who was renting his house at the time, says it was Paul who persuaded him to make the effort to buy somewhere instead. It was pretty much the best financial advice he had ever been given.

Back in Britain Paul had decided to put straight acting on the back burner. The Paul Savage who appears in the credits to *In the Name of the Father* in 1993 would not take on any further work. Paul finally felt financially strong enough to give Lily Savage his full attention. He and Brendan talked endlessly about the right strategy for the act. The live shows and the associated videos such as *Paying the Rent* were becoming increasingly lavish and lucrative. Paul knew he could probably spend the rest of his life making a great living as a touring act. But something told him he should take things further. He still wanted to move up a gear and make it back on to mainstream television – if only to prove that he could. Over the past few years so many people had told him that an act like Lily Savage was perfect for the pubs and might just about make it into the theatres, but would only ever succeed on national television as a one-off novelty act. Every time he'd heard the claims Paul had wanted to prove them all wrong. He still did.

So he and Brendan kept on following up every small expression of interest from television producers and casting agents. They now had show reels and a stack of top-quality reviews to offer as proof of how safe a bet Lily had become. And in October 1994 they made what felt like another big breakthrough: Lily tottered out of the wings at BBC Centre on to the set of *The Steve Wright People Show*. She got more than her fair share of laughs from the start – not least in an early sketch when she was paired up with a so-called dating expert who was testing out his chat-up lines on her. The first batch came in a supermarket.

'Are you cooking for two tonight?' Lily was asked suggestively.

'I am actually. I've got a tapeworm,' she fired back.

'Maybe I could kiss you under the moonlight,' her hopeful suitor followed up.

'I wouldn't kiss you under general anaesthetic,' she replied.

The routines meant Lily was soon asked back for another appearance on the show, triggering what the comedian turned writer and broadcaster Simon Fanshawe said was a fascinating and important moment. 'I still remember the second time Lily appeared on Steve Wright's show,' he says. 'He kissed her and encountered her as an entirely believable character. Because, despite the violent drag and the metric tonnes of make-up, Lily is in some way real. She's not a man in a frock. She doesn't belong in the rugby-players-in-dresses-for-charity strand of British drag, or to Danny La Rue's camp deceit. She is drawn from a tradition of working-class humour whose patron saints are Ken Dodd and his bizarre world of Knotty Ash and Les Dawson with his rambling family reminiscences.' He goes on to explain that as he talks, you realise that Paul has a compulsion to describe. 'Images fall over themselves in the rush to get out and they summon up a world of poverty and resilience. Where Lily excels is painting these wild, live, florid, hilarious pictures, almost rococo in their embellishments.'

Paul was thrilled with the compliments and particularly pleased to be put in the same category as the likes of Ken Dodd and Les Dawson. And he agreed with Simon that British pub and television humour had to be rooted at the bottom end of the social scale. The likes of Hugh Grant could make it in Hollywood, where an idealised view of the landed gentry still got bums on seats. But jokes had to come from somewhere else.

'There's nothing really funny about an upper-class world but there's something very funny about an outside lav and getting your apron strings caught in the mangle,' Paul says with a twinkle in his eye. There was also plenty that was funny about Lily's ever-changing act – a fact that was recognised when Lily was nominated as Top Live Stand-up Comedian and Top Television Comedy Newcomer at the year's British Comedy Awards.

The BBC were keen to keep finding work for Lily, and she was brought in to be a half-serious social commentator on the BBC2 show *Life Swaps*. The six-part series was ahead of its time, an early combination of *Faking It* and *Wife Swap* that never quite got the ratings or the buzz it deserved. On one of the first shows Radio 4's *Woman's Hour* reporter Tessa Williams swapped lives and jobs with Stuart Qualtrough of the *Sunday Sport*. In the process, she found herself writing stories along the lines of 'Woman Gives Birth To Oven Ready Chickens' while Stuart, who had been schooled on the *Sun*, found himself researching a middle-aged woman's guide to pregnancy. Friends, homes and hobbies were also switched – while Lily watched and commented on every move the participants made.

Producer Nick Crombie says Lily was the perfect choice for the role. 'She has an acute sense of social detail and class behaviour,' he said. She was also hilariously funny and had a great time getting to know the show's participants and nosing around in their lives. But after filming the first six episodes, low ratings meant the show never got a second series.

Lily, though, was on a roll. Jonathan Ross had become a big fan and was championing her for as many shows as he could think of. She got top billing at gay rights group Stonewall's Equality Show. The show was staged at the Albert Hall in London, another venue Paul had always dreamed of playing. Then, just two days later, he was interviewed by Gloria Hunniford for *Pebble Mill*. Backstage at both the Albert Hall and the BBC studios, Paul found himself in extraordinary company. 'It's mad. This week I've met Elton and Sting and sat on a couch with Ivana, Lulu and Kylie. I also shouted at Richard Gere by mistake, accusing him of not zipping my dress up fully because I thought he was from the wardrobe department.'

Paul, loving it, had scaled the first-name only world that had always seemed so elusive. And more dreams were to come true in the next few months. In November 1994 he stole the show when he got a bit part on *Brookside*, a joy for a lifelong soap fan. The latest plot had seen Barry Grant and Max Farnham trying to join the restaurant business, and both characters had inadvertently invited a different celebrity guest to open it. So Lily Savage was up against Lloyd Grossman – and Lily stole the show. Amazingly for such a tightly run soap, Paul was allowed to ad-lib his way through most of his scenes.

He loved it – as did the cast and the audiences. 'I just decided to let Lily enjoy herself and lord it over Lloyd Grossman. Fortunately, he took it all as good fun,' he said afterwards.

And appearing on *Brookside* wasn't the last iconic television gig of the year. Lily was about to be a guest presenter on *Top of the Pops* before winning an early shot at daytime television – the market Paul would dominate in his own right nearly a decade later.

Back then, Lily had Judy Finnigan and Richard Madeley in stitches on the *This Morning* sofa and would become one of the show's most regular and popular guests. 'Lily brings a wonderfully barbed edge to a horribly bland medium,' was how one critic saw it. What other critics commented on was the fact that Lily was far from a one-trick pony. Yes, she told and re-told her favourite anecdotes on a regular basis. But then Frank Sinatra sang *My Way* every time the fridge door opened and Cher has a farewell tour every fifteen minutes, Paul would say. More seriously, he knew that audiences would be disappointed if some of their favourite stories didn't get told. And he always had plenty of new material to add to the mix.

'Where do you get it all from?' the reporter Brian Reade asked him in the dressing room of Croydon's Fairfield Halls in the spring of 1995 when Lily was back on tour. Paul admitted it was from some pretty unconventional places. 'If I see women like Lily in markets I still sidle up to them and listen,' he said. 'I know them. I can picture their houses – bathroom and kitchen spotless and everywhere else rotten. I'll always have a soft spot for the Lilys of this world.'

His fans were also unwittingly keeping Lily fresh. Night after night people would find a way to his dressing room or wait at the stage door after his shows and talk about their own problems rather than Lily's performance. They might tell him how one small part of his act had rung true, how some throwaway line had struck a chord and made them reassess what they were doing or where they were going. 'Sometimes, when I was out of my costumes, I would ask them, "What did you tell me that for?" And they would say, "I didn't tell you. I told Lily." It meant she was more alive than anyone had ever imagined.'

The year's tour, which began in Croydon, had been due to last for a gruelling two months. But as Lily fever mounted, and even the 2,000-seater venues sold out, a third month was added – the tour would now take in 36 dates across Britain, Ireland and the Channel Islands. Fortunately for him, Paul loved being on the road. He says he often prefers hotel beds to his own and frequently feels a pang of regret when he has to check out and return to what passes for normality back home. Always happy to embrace the unfashionable and defy conventions, he says one of his favourite venues is Torquay where he took tea at the Imperial Hotel long before he could ever afford to stay there.

What Paul also liked about his latest tour was that it

gave the lie to the conservatives who still thought his act was too racy to make the mainstream. Back in 1995 it turned out that some of Lily's biggest fans were pensioners. 'They turn up by the coach load and none of them is under 60 and I love it because they're not your typical sniffy, snobby comedy audience analysing your material and too afraid to really laugh at it. I go on about hypothermia and VE Day. I tell them that pensioners don't want to be sitting in an air raid shelter listening to Vera Lynn because they've done all that. I tell them they just want to go out and get drunk and get laid, plastic hip or no plastic hip, and they roar. People forget that old people have seen it all.'

Women were his other core audience – not least because they saw Lily as someone who told the truth about the men in their lives. One night on tour in Birmingham, for example, Paul says he stood in the wings and could almost feel the atmosphere and the anticipation. 'The whole audience seemed to be made up of hard-bitten, bleach-haired divorcees and as soon as I started talking about fellas you could almost hear them muttering: "Go on, Lil, rip into 'em!" Women appreciate Lily because she says all the things about men and life that they would like to say but daren't. I talk about real life and women respond to that. Men get the hump because they know I've got a foot in both camps. I say things about men's secrets that I shouldn't.'

And while some critics seem to feel that all drag acts are somehow mocking women, Paul would prove that he had nothing but respect for them. He refused to portray Lily as a victim of men and hoped that her example could do some good in the world. An example came when Paul met theatre boss Cameron Mackintosh at the London Palladium. The musical *Oliver!* had just been named as the theatre's longest running show and Paul told the producer that Lily would be perfect in the lead role of Nancy – but only after an important change. 'You wouldn't catch me singing *As Long As He Needs Me* after getting a black eye. If they changed it to Nancy belting Bill Sykes rather than the other way around and him singing that song in casualty, then I'd be up for it,' Paul declared, with the kind of spirit that left his female fans cheering.

After joining in the celebrations at the Palladium, Paul headed to an equally prestigious London theatre to film another big one-off show of his own. *Lily Savage: Live and Outrageous at the Garrick Theatre* would be another successful video release, and the highlight of the night was a brilliant spoof of Torvill and Dean's Bolero routine – with Christopher Dean on stage trying to turn Lily into Jayne. It wasn't pretty, the fans said. But it was eye-wateringly funny.

At the same time, things were stirring again on the television front. The original series of *Viva Cabaret!* was being repeated on Channel 4 while a new series, *Live from the Lilydrome*, filmed in a working mens' club in Blackpool, was being planned for Saturday nights. In the film world the proof that you have succeeded comes when you get your name above the title on the posters. In television the proof comes when your name is in the title. So while *Live from the Lilydrome* is barely remembered today, it meant a huge amount to Paul at the time.

So was everything rosy in Paul and Lily's garden that year? It should have been. Money was rolling in, celebrity fans were desperate to meet the man who was making everyone laugh, and his professional diary was getting booked up almost a year in advance. But in some quarters a mini-backlash was starting to brew. Amazingly enough, some of his earlier fans from the pubs were accusing Paul of selling out. Many of the acts Lily had once performed alongside were still stuck in the same south London clubs. Friends told him how their latest banter had them rolling their heavily made-up eyes in disgust at the way Lily had supposedly sold her soul.

To his credit Paul wasn't having any of it. He didn't accept the criticism and he wasn't shy of telling people why. 'I explain to them that I've done nearly ten years on the factory floor and now I feel I deserve a shot in the office,' he said. 'I used to worry whether I could afford a train fare back to Liverpool. I remember times when I couldn't go out. I've been broke, so yes, being able to pay my bills now is fantastic and I won't apologise for it.'

What Paul could also have said was that he still did more than his fair share of fee-free charity and benefit performances. He was a stalwart fundraiser for several HIV and Aids charities and was also taking an interest in several other good causes, looking after everyone from the homeless to carers. Whatever they said about Lily Savage, no one would ever be able to say that Paul O'Grady had forgotten his roots. And if you needed any more evidence you needed only to visit him at home.

CHAPTER FIVE
The Big Breakfast

'The first thing I saw when I arrived was a Beware Of The Cat doormat,' says journalist and author Imogen Edwards-Jones, who visited Paul's flat for an interview as his career finally took off. This wasn't to be the only item that raised eyebrows in the tiny one-bedroom flat.

Imogen remembers acres of leopard-skin and a range of glow-in-the-dark transparent plastic Virgin Marys – plus what she described as whole armies of ducks flying across the walls. Then there was the fish tank in the bathroom filled with soaps from almost every hotel Paul or his friends had ever stayed in. Plastic Disney characters perched on picture rails, window sills and any other surface. There was a drunk-looking stuffed raven slumped next to a voodoo snake wand. In the bedroom there were leopard-skin sheets, a leopard-skin duvet cover, leopard-skin curtains and leopard-skin wallpaper. The tiny bedside cabinet was full of Rennies, there was a Noddy clock, an astro lamp, a 1940s radio and a gap where his Teasmade used to sit (it scalded him every morning and he ended up bashing it with the baseball bat that he keeps under the bed for security reasons). The word 'eclectic' had been made to describe a home like this.

On a softer note, many of the illustrations and cartoons that Paul had drawn as a boy in Birkenhead were now framed and put in pride of place on the walls of his narrow, equally crowded hallway. Paul happily admits that the whole flat was ridiculously cramped. He had more than 3,000 video tapes stacked up wherever there was room – mainly of old American films and long-forgotten episodes of *Coronation Street*. Getting into the tiny kitchen involved squeezing past a never-used StairMaster machine that Paul had unaccountably ordered from a television shopping channel in Amsterdam and had regretted ever since. But since he reckoned all he ever had in the kitchen were mushy peas and Bird's custard no one really felt that the machine was in the way.

What made matters worse was Paul's suspicion that he wasn't always living alone. He reckoned he could hear rats scurrying around at night and got the fright of his life one morning when he walked into the bathroom to see one staring back at him from the toilet. Neighbours said they were swimming up through the sewage pipes in search of food in the flats' kitchens. So why exactly was Paul still squashed into a tiny council flat in a mansion block in Vauxhall, the south London suburb that continued to defy all attempts at gentrification?

One reason was that Lily was keeping him so busy he didn't have the time to look for anywhere new. Another was that it was easier to stick with what he knew – he had been in Victoria Mansions for thirteen years and wasn't sure he could uproot himself. But the final reason was that Paul continued to be a worrier. Yes, he was earning huge amounts of money at last, but he feared that splashing out on some flash pad somewhere else might just tempt fate. If he bought a new home, the work might dry up and he would be unable to pay the bills. Then, suddenly, dear old Vicky Mansions wouldn't have looked so bad. His Birkenhead upbringing had a lot to answer for, he would tell friends who thought his superstitions and cautions were ridiculous. What Paul didn't know was that the work was far from drying up. A unique vacancy was about to crop up on Channel 4. It was a vacancy for a job Lily had been born to fill.

One of the biggest television phenomena of the 1990s was Channel 4's *Big Breakfast* – though Paul happily admits he was rarely awake early enough to watch it. Bob Geldof had created the show for his Planet 24 production company and it was fast turning into one of the biggest star-makers in the country. The show's first presenters, Chris Evans and Gaby Roslin, had become instant celebrities, and Mark Lamarr had joined the mainstream in his 'on-the-road' role.

But in terms of attracting headlines, Bob's wife Paula Yates was hard to beat. For three years she had been the most unconventional celebrity interviewer in the country. Guests joined her on the big red double bed where her flirtatious questioning soon became legendary. And it seemed like the whole country was open-mouthed when it was revealed that she was having an affair with a man she had actually met on the *Big Breakfast* bed, INXS star Michael Hutchence. When Paula decided to leave Bob for Michael, she knew she would have to leave the programme as well. So as the scandal rumbled on there was a vacancy on what was billed as 'television's favourite bed'. Who would lie in it now that Paula had gone?

The producers knew they needed someone fearless. Despite her flirtatious manner, Paula had never shied from asking the tough questions, so they didn't want to replace her with some shrinking violet who would stick to a PR-approved script. It might be breakfast television, but Planet 24 still wanted the sparks to fly. They also wanted a replacement interviewer who would get the newspapers interested, someone who would get people tuning in even if the guests themselves weren't always at the top of the A-list. Very few of the established chat show names angling for the role could promise all of this. Looking back it's easy to see why Lily Savage got the call.

'Oh my God.' Paul looked out at the silver stretch limo that the *Big Breakfast* producers had rented to drive him to the launch press conference at its east London studios. The four-week trial run of *Lie-in With Lily* needed to start with a bang and Paul wasn't going to miss a trick. Lily was top to toe in a signature leopard-skin outfit (with matching umbrella) and she told anyone who cared to ask that she was doused in her favourite perfume, Flame of Llandudno. Waving, smiling and sneering at a group of autograph-hunters when the car arrived at its destination, Lily tottered in to face the biggest media scrum of her life. She loved it, Paul joked afterwards. And she gave great value.

'Who do you want to interview first?' one reporter asked her.

She picked rugby's Will Carling, the man who had just led England's World Cup win over Australia. 'I want to have Will on the bed, especially after he said he can't cross his legs because his thighs are too big,' she said with a lasciviousness that was pure Paula. What Lily refused to do was to criticise her predecessor on the show. 'I like her. The only thing I've got against her are those daft names she's given her kids – Fifi Trixibelle and Cabbage.'

How Lily would cope with the pre-dawn starts on the *Big Breakfast* was another matter. 'She'll have to watch *Coronation Street* and be in bed by 9pm,' Paul joked to Planet 24 staff after the press conference was over. What he didn't know was that breakfast television was no laughing matter. Long-term presenters such as Lorraine Kelly, Fiona Phillips and Eamonn Holmes say getting enough sleep soon becomes a personal obsession. They need to work hard to protect themselves from picking up bugs and viruses and can easily feel that their lives are out of sync with the rest of the world. The early nights and relentless early morning calls can put huge pressures on relationships. Breakfast television can give you a wonderful platform as a presenter. But it can carry a high price behind the scenes.

For Paul, the downsides of the job seemed unimportant. His original contract was only for four weeks, after all, with other guest interviewers like Vanessa Feltz also being lined up for trial stints on the famous bed. And in the summer of 1995 all Paul could really think about was his pay packet. He was collecting £5,000 a week, easily the best earnings of his career. To no one's real surprise *Lie-in With Lily* was a hit. So when the trial run ended she was signed up for an extended and even better-rewarded stay in the early morning boudoir. This was the big time and while he wanted to enjoy every minute, Paul was determined to live it on his terms.

'Paul – the cigarette! Paul!'

Almost every morning in the *Big Breakfast* studios, Paul would see the same looks of horror on the faces of the production staff. Because almost every morning he would still be holding a cigarette as the theme music played and his part of the show was counted in. Then every morning, as the cameras turned to him he would ditch the cigarette and start talking into the camera as if to the manner born. 'I kept them on their toes,' he joked afterwards, loving it each morning when total panic was replaced by relief on the faces of all around him. He was on the edge, as usual, and he felt at home there.

Paul also loved getting such close access to so many star guests. With some two million viewers and a 30 per cent share of the breakfast audience, the *Big Breakfast* was able to attract A-listers from America as well as Britain. So Hollywood and music names who had never heard of Lily Savage would get quite a wake-up call when they walked on to the set. Paul had long since made a vow that he would ignore any instructions his guests' PRs or advisers gave before the interviews. No questions or topics would be off-limits for Lily – because Paul felt he owed that to the viewers. 'I just decided to ask the questions I knew the average punter would want to ask. And thankfully I didn't meet anyone who wasn't a good sport about it all.'

And as his show became established Paul proved he was one of the best sports of all – not least when he stood in the studio gardens at 6.30am one morning dressed as a cowgirl with a chicken under his arm singing "Islands In The Stream" with Kenny Rogers. It was one of those television moments that was always going to be a classic. Back on her bed in the studio, Lily's characteristic ramblings would leave the production staff and viewers in stitches – even if some of her American guests were left unsure of exactly what or who she was talking about. 'Yes, I was approached to take over as Bet Gilroy in *Coronation Street* but I had to turn it down. I've got another major project underway – *The Valerie Singleton Story*. I play the young Val,' Lily boasted one morning, as her guest struggled to get a word in edgeways.

The problem for Paul as his role on the *Big Breakfast* became more established was that he hadn't allowed his lifestyle to catch up with him. He refused to cancel any of the late-night engagements he had already signed, and was too cautious to always turn down new ones. Plus, of course, he still wanted to go out drinking with his mates, not least because he had a constant new source of solid gold gossip to pass on from all the guests at Channel 4. All his life, Paul has said that waking up is the worst moment of his day, even if he hasn't been up late the night before. 'It's traumatic, like a near-death experience every morning,' he jokes. 'What I want is time for a good Birkenhead breakfast – ten ciggies and a pot of tea while I sit in silence like a pitbull, growling.' With this in mind, breakfast television was hardly the ideal place for him to work. And after three months on the breakfast bed it was clear that Paul was being spread too thinly. Very soon the cracks would start to show.

'I don't want to do this.' It was 4.30am and the *Big Breakfast* car was waiting outside Paul's flat to take him to the studio. But that particular morning Paul thought he couldn't go. He was rocking backwards and forwards on the edge of his bed, tears funnelling down his face, feeling so weak he could barely stand up. He had been out partying the night before and had had next to no sleep. 'I can't live like this,' he muttered under his breath as he forced himself out of his house. Cigarettes and can after can of Red Bull were becoming the new tools of his trade, the essential items that got him off the edge of his bed and into the Channel 4 car every morning. Many was the evening when he had just two hours' sleep – and he dreaded going into the hair and make-up sessions at the studio the following morning.

What was sapping Paul's energy even more was the knowledge that things would get a lot worse before they got better. Everyone at the *Big Breakfast* was warning their new colleague to slow down and look after himself. But he had secretly signed up for yet another draining challenge. The timing was appalling. But he was going to star in his first West End musical. He would be performing on stage until long past all the other breakfast presenters had gone to bed and it was going to test his strength to the limit.

The show in question was typically bizarre. *Prisoner Cell Block H*, the cult Australian television series that made the just-revived *Crossroads* look like Chekhov, had been adapted for the stage. And it had been put to music. From the moment he heard about it Paul knew he simply couldn't turn down the chance to star in the show.

'It's so over the top, it's fantastic. It's got angst,

intrigue, power struggles, lagging on your mates – all set in a women's prison. How can it fail?' he joked when friends said he was crazy. 'It could fail because it's a musical – and because you can't sing,' Paul was told time and again. And he couldn't deny it. He reckoned he could do a passable Elvis after a few drinks but he remembers his mother would always say his singing voice sounded 'like coal under a cellar door'. Not quite the stuff of an Olivier award, but that wasn't going to put Paul off, especially as he knew he was going to be playing alongside one of his trash television heroines. Maggie Kirkpatrick, the Australian actress who had been in almost all of *Cell Block's* extraordinary 692 television episodes, had been flown in from Australia to reprise her role as the power-mad warden Joan 'The Freak' Ferguson. Even if the show sank without trace, it promised to be an hilarious experience backstage, Paul said. The only problem, of course, was that it was going to be so hugely demanding.

That summer Paul continued to force himself out of bed at 4.30am for the live *Big Breakfast* broadcasts. Then he headed into central London to rehearse for *Prisoner* all afternoon before working on his next video release in a Soho studio until past midnight. His daily cigarette intake, he said, was approaching an all-time high. His energy levels were at an all-time low.

The journalist and author Justine Picardie, who met him backstage at the Old Vic theatre during those rehearsals, says she got a shock when she walked into the room. 'He looked as unlike Lily Savage as you could possibly imagine. A tall thin man, grey-haired and grey-faced with exhaustion. He wears black jeans and a plain white shirt and his voice as is understated as his appearance.'

Funnily enough, theatre studies student Janice Scott, who researched the capital's comedy acts for her dissertation, says Justine had hit the nail on the head. She says one of the most common words ever used to describe Paul and Lily in the mid- to late-1990s was not outrageous, flamboyant or theatrical – it was exhausted. 'When you read all the newspaper articles about Paul from those days, it just leaps out at you how tired everyone said Paul had become,' she says. 'People say he was drained, listless, pale. He was the most entertaining person in the industry back then. But being Paul O'Grady didn't seem as if it was a great deal of fun.'

Little wonder then that Paul was desperate to surround himself with as many home comforts as possible – however unorthodox some of them might be. Journalist Christy Campbell went backstage into Paul's dressing room just before *Prisoner*'s opening night and found a packet of Silk Cut, a bottle of Lourdes water, a box of tea-bags, several industrial-sized packs of cold cream and a sea of good luck cards on every possible surface. But it didn't do the trick. Paul came down with a nasty cold just before opening night – but he refused to pull out. His entertainment mantra had always been that the show had to go on, so he gargled with some soluble aspirin and took to the stage as planned. A big celebrity turn-out at the

979-seat Queen's Theatre on Shaftsbury Avenue had turned opening night into a media scrum – and fortunately the whole audience seemed to whoop, cheer, boo and hiss with abandon as the cast threw dignity to the winds and hammed it up for all they were worth.

The critics, not surprisingly, had no idea how to take it. 'If there was an award for the tackiest, campest musical in town this show would walk it. Imagine a cross between *The Rocky Horror Show* and *Acorn Antiques* and you will get some idea of what's on offer,' the *Telegraph* informed its middle-England readers. 'The acting is dreadful and as well as delivering their lines with a woodenness that verges on the heroic, the cast have to expend considerable effort in holding up the wobbly scenery.' But while the show might have been given the thumbs down, Paul himself got the *Telegraph*'s official seal of approval later in the same review. 'Thin as a beanpole and sporting a wig like peroxide candy floss, Savage has a fine sense of timing, a wonderful expression of indignant pursed-lipped outrage, while her put-downs, delivered in thickest Scouse, would make Danny La Rue blush. He richly deserves his star billing,' the paper concluded.

Other reviewers were equally kind, treating the show like an early pantomime and seeing any faults as part of its charm. 'So kitsch it's hip' was how the *Independent on Sunday* put it. 'There is a riot going on in Cell Block H and you would be mad to miss it,' the *Mirror* concluded. What gave Paul a shock backstage was that it wasn't just the British press and audiences who wanted to speak to him.

'Aren't you just taking the piss out of Down Under with this show?'

The cameras were rolling in Paul's dressing room after one of the first week's performances as he was being interviewed by Australian television. He was giving as good value as ever.

'Absolutely not. I adore Oz – I was brought up in Britain on Australian television shows. And I just had a dream about Skippy the bush kangaroo. I had a vision that he is living outside Melbourne like Norma Desmond in *Sunset Boulevard*, wearing a turban and saying, "I am big. It's the bush that got smaller."'

'Paul, there's some other people who want to talk to you,' one of the theatre staff said when the Australian cameras were switched off. 'They're Russian. The Russians love the show. They want to know if we could take it there on tour.'

'Well, after playing the Royal Vauxhall Tavern for eight years I think I can do anything,' Paul told her, before waving the fans in and signing autographs for all of them.

For all the late-night laughs at the Queen's Theatre, the fact that Paul had to be back in the *Big Breakfast* studios before dawn most days continued to put a huge strain on him. And what made it so much harder were Lily's still outrageous costumes. If he had been one of the jeans and T-shirt comedians Paul had been competing against all those years ago, then his daily routines would at least have been a little shorter and easier. As it was, he had to be dressed in a series of increasingly uncomfortable costumes for up to sixteen hours a day. He also felt the pressure always to be funny and on form, because once he was dressed up it was impossible to be anonymous or hide in the background. Even mad dashes across London in the back of a taxi turned into mini-ordeals as Lily tended to be spotted by passing lorry drivers and bus passengers. When traffic was slow, Paul could find himself posing for pictures and signing autographs in the few brief moments he had hoped to spend catching up on sleep.

So it was little wonder that he was always trying to find somewhere else to close the door and crash, even if it was for just fifteen minutes at a time. His dressing room became an essential refuge and Paul was also seeking help in any form it could come, something he is happy to joke about now. 'I became very Janis Joplin,' he remembers. 'The doctor would come to my dressing room and give me a B12 shot that would keep me going for three days.'

What nearly knocked him for six, however, were the real challenges he was about to face in his private life. And as a television personality he was going to find out just how public this could be.

The challenges came as he tried to build a relationship with the daughter he had hardly seen in nearly twenty years. Sharyn had grown up into a slim and beautiful woman and wanted to know more about her dad. But while doing so she would have to face the might of the British tabloids, which had only just found out she existed. 'Transvestite TV comic Lily Savage has been hiding two big secrets ... he is married and has a love child,' screamed the front page of the *Sunday Mirror* in the autumn of 1995. Two of the paper's reporters had tracked down Theresa Fernandes and decided they had struck gold with their story. Theresa refused to say a bad word against Paul, just as she has steadfastly refused to do ever since. But while she wasn't the mother of his child Theresa couldn't deny that Paul was in fact a father. So the tabloids were determined to keep on digging.

ARE YOU LILY'S DAUGHTER? the *Sunday Mirror* asked in huge type at the end of its 'exclusive' story about the comic's past. 'Or do you know who she is? Contact the newsdesk and don't worry about the cost – we'll call you straight back.' It was tacky stuff but readers were lapping it up and the papers knew that the first one to find Paul's secret daughter would see sales soar – at least for a day. The pressure from the tabloids couldn't really have come at a worse time for either Paul or Sharyn. Both admit that they have had their ups and downs since they met up when she was a teenager.

'You're an unfit father!' Paul remembers Sharyn yelling at him after one tense early meeting, never quite sure if she was joking.

'I didn't want a child at seventeen and you came along,' he would rail back, fully aware that he sounded like a seventeen-year-old all over again.

In their calmer moments, Paul was the first to admit how hard all this must have been on Sharyn. 'To suddenly have this strange man who dressed up as a woman to deal with. Just imagine how that would have been to cope with when you were just a teenager.' The fact that Sharyn did cope is something he says is a credit to both her and to her mother Diane. Fortunately for her, Sharyn seemed to have somehow inherited her father's quick wit and would never have a problem fighting her corner when the heat was on. Paul laughed and was secretly proud when he got Father's Day cards laced with the sarcasm and cynicism that marked her out as an O'Grady in nature if not in name. 'Thanks for being such a wonderful father,' she wrote in one card. And instead of being hurt Paul loved and admired her for it.

He also accepted that he had a lot of making up to do. 'I think Sharyn would have loved a pipe and slippers by the fire sort of dad, and look what she got: a male Elsie Tanner. I look at her and I think: "You could do better than me." I was never there to wipe her nose, to read her bedtime stories or tell her how clever she was. I was never there for her at all. And while I try to make up for that now, I know I never can. But I think now we can have a happy ending.'

As part of their very late getting-to-know-you act Paul threw a twenty-first birthday party for Sharyn in London that year, with her mum Diane as the other guest of honour. Despite the fact that the events that had brought them all together resembled the worst plots from a soap opera, the evening passed without any tension.

As had Paul's other big party of the year, the belated 40th birthday party he threw for himself in a London theatre. Paul had rented a mini-bus to bring the Merseyside contingent down and everyone had a ball mingling with the likes of Sir Ian McKellen and former *EastEnders* star Michael Cashman. Despite the best efforts of the tabloids, the complications of his private life and the gruelling routine of the *Big Breakfast* and *Prisoner C Block H*, Paul was looking forward to his 40s – though he joked that Lily had taken the news about her age very badly.

Paul hoped to appease her with the news that Channel 4 was showing one of the updated *Paying the Rent* shows on New Year's Eve – and that both ITV and the BBC were also competing to win her for some prime-time programmes in 1996. But before any of that could come off, Paul was hoping a change of scene would give him a new lease of life. *Prisoner Cell Block H* was going on a national tour just as Paul was due a short break from his *Big Breakfast* commitments. Paul was thrilled that he could join everyone on the ride.

Within weeks it was clear that he had made the right decision. His skin and eyes were looking brighter as he escaped the worries and pressures of London. Friends and colleagues said they could see the difference in him straight away. Less early starts, more sleep and better food were doing him a world of good. For his part, Paul says being back in one of his beloved hotel rooms was a tonic in its own right. 'You've no worries when your world is in a bag. No phone calls, no hassle. The only thing you have to do is answer your fan mail and pay the gas bills now and again.' His new dog, Buster, loved exploring new places as well, though finding dog-friendly hotels was sometimes a challenge – and he said stopping Buster from running off with the cast's purses and tights in the dressing room could also be easier said than done.

As the stresses faded away and the *Prisoner* crew started to thrive on the good reactions they got on tour, Paul found he had the energy to start partying again. And in co-star Maggie Kirkpatrick he found a great friend and perfect new partner in crime. They might have been behind bars on stage, but they were in front of them most nights. Paul loved it.

'I had to try and be asleep by eight for the *Big Breakfast* and I had forgotten what a good night out was like. Maggie and I make Gazza and the England football team look like *The Waltons*,' he joked about some of their big nights out. 'Last week we were in Liverpool, which Maggie has renamed Liverdamage. Next week the show moves to Edinburgh and I'm dreading it. It's one of my favourite places but it could be the death of me. Last time I was there I was singing karaoke in a pub until 6am. I try to stick to cider but sometimes Maggie tempts me with whisky. There have been days when I have woken up and wanted to be buried alive.'

Cracking jokes, buying drinks and having fun. By the time Paul and the *Prisoner* cast hit Scotland everyone was on top form. 'Liking Paul certainly isn't difficult,' said *Daily Mirror* writer Steve King, who met the newly relaxed man in his dressing room the night the show moved across to Glasgow. Leaving London had clearly been the right thing for Paul to do. But with the *Prisoner* tour entering its final few weeks he knew it would soon be time to head back down south. It turned out that Lily Savage had been badly missed. Paul was about to be even busier than ever.

CHAPTER SIX

The Good Times

Paul was led through the rabbit warren of corridors in the old LWT Tower on the south bank of the Thames. The building, now called The London Studios, was where so many of the classic shows from the 1970s and 1980s had been filmed. Its main studio was big and flexible enough for all the huge set-piece variety shows that Paul had always loved. Latterly it was where all the big *An Evening With* specials were filmed – the celebrity-filled nights that showcased comedians like Dame Edna Everage, Bob Monkhouse, Joan Rivers and Victoria Wood, and where they had recently started to honour singers such as Shirley Bassey.

In April 1996, Paul could hardly believe he was in the same gilded company. He was heading to the same vast sound stage to record a variation on the theme, *An Evening With Lily Savage*. It was pretty much the ultimate proof of how far Lily had travelled from that tiny corner stage in the Elephant & Castle pub. But would she really shine in such a strong spotlight?

From the moment *An Evening With Lily Savage* had first been mentioned, Paul had decided to work on his own scripts. Teams of professional writers were made available to him, people who would work in secret and never take any credit away from their employers. But Paul wasn't ready to trust his baby to anyone else. He also wanted to make sure that he had plenty of his new famous friends in the audience, though this would ultimately cause problems of its own. One of Lily's key selling points was that she was tough as nails and insufferably rude to her audiences. But while it was easy to let rip when he was heckled by a stranger in a pub, it didn't seem so easy when he faced one of his new pals on national television.

After such a long stint confined to the *Big Breakfast* bed and playing a role in *Prisoner Cell Block H* Paul was also worried that his live act might have become rusty. The final problem on the day the show was filmed was that, friend or not, the celebrity guests didn't always act the way Paul wanted them to. He stood fuming in the wings as they milled around chatting when they were supposed to be taking their seats and getting ready for his big entrance. When they took even longer to settle after a short break halfway through the recording, he felt like rushing out on to the stage to scream at them. And for a while he feared it might have made better television if he had.

The show was filmed and edited by the end of April. But it would end up sitting on ITV's shelves for more than six months before finally being aired in November. Everyone assured Paul that this was simply a scheduling issue, an essential delay if they wanted to get the maximum autumn audience for the work. But the nervous, superstitious side of Paul couldn't quite believe it. His insecurities would flood back as he worried that there might be a more sinister reason. Had the channel lost its nerve? Had he lost his edge? Was his biggest break to end up on the cutting room floor surrounded by some very public humiliation?

As it turned out *An Evening With Lily Savage* would win ITV one of its biggest audiences of the year when it was finally shown on the second Wednesday in November. It was scheduled against a hugely well-promoted double bill of *Absolutely Fabulous* on the BBC. But Lily won an extraordinary 11.2 million viewers – nearly three million more than Edina and Patsy could attract to the Beeb. The critics, though, seemed to take a very different view.

'Programme-makers Carlton referred to Lily Savage as: "The first lady of British comedy". In their dreams. The only things Lily comes first in are bawdiness and bad taste. She makes Dame Edna look like a shrinking violet and the height of sophistication. No wonder Paul

O'Grady never shows his face,' wrote the *Daily Mirror*'s Tony Purnell. He was equally critical of the celebrity audience. 'Most of the "in" crowd who attended the show became the "out" crowd a long time ago. Rod Hull without Emu, Robbie Williams without Take That, Torvill and Dean without ice. The faces in the crowd really were those who would turn up at the opening of an envelope.'

A tiny number of viewers had also rung up to complain about some of Paul's language and the adult themes in his anecdotes. Then a very unlikely critic stepped up to join them – it was Danny la Rue, the grande dame of drag. He said he totally sympathised with anyone who thought Paul's risqué humour was a high-heeled step too far for prime-time television. 'Nowadays I see myself as an alternative, alternative comic. Alternative to all the filth the so-called alternative comedians do. I would never crack risqué jokes in front of children,' La Rue declared. It was stilettos at dawn, as one showbusiness reporter wrote when the row hit the papers.

But amid all the controversy there had been some great comic moments in Lily's *Evening*. One great line came about when actor Dean Sullivan, Jimmy Corkhill in *Brookside*, was picked out by the camera crew. 'Dean, what a sportsman. He's the man who taught me how to fence,' Lily said. 'I don't mean with a sword. I mean the removal of stolen gear.'

Lily then begged Robbie Williams to give up the young girlfriend at his side and to cuddle up with her instead.

'Robbie, have you ever considered an older woman? Stewing steak instead of flash fried?'

Paul was to get the last laugh, when the critics were long forgotten. *An Evening With Lily Savage* won Best Entertainment Programme at the National Television Awards in 1997. All the stress and worry had been worthwhile. And as the dust settled, ITV even put together a £250,000 deal to ensure all of Lily's next shows were made with them.

Amazingly, Paul wasn't entirely sure if he should sign it. One of the first shows the channel offered would have had a prime 8pm Wednesday night slot. But Paul took a deep breath and said he couldn't do it. 'At that stage of my career I knew it would have diluted me. Lily still talked about sex, drugs and shoplifting. She talked about bailiffs and the police. If I couldn't do that, then what's the point? I would have been drawn into the world of "Light Entertainment" and become Danny La Rue.'

In a year or two's time Paul thought Lily would be ready for this kind of gear change. But for now he was ready to take a long-term view and play to her strengths. It wasn't as if he hadn't been working flat out all year either – not for nothing had he just acquired the new nickname Hurricane Lily! In the summer, he had been performing in Blackpool, one of his favourite northern cities, for a sold-out sixteen-week run at the North Pier theatre.

Those four months at the seaside were another lifesaver for Paul – because the moment he arrived for his first rehearsal he felt good. Blackpool might not offer much in the way of genuine glamour, but Paul had always felt at home there. 'The first time I ever went I was about twenty-two and I remember going out for a walk along the front and spotting Janette from The Krankies. I rushed up to her and said I was a huge fan. She said she was going for a cup of tea and would I like to join her. I was a complete stranger but that's just the kind of relaxed place Blackpool is. Good things happen there.'

They certainly did that summer. Paul had the pop star and old pal Sonia as well as the classical singer Russell Watson among his supporting cast, and *The Lily Savage Show* got some of the best reviews of his career. After a month-long break at the end of it, he was back in town headlining at the Blackpool Opera House for *Lily's Christmas Cracker* alongside Sean Maguire and another old friend, Brenda Gilhooly as Gayle Tuesday.

As usual, Paul had set himself a relentless pace – so by the time Christmas came around he was hoping for a few moments of peace and quiet. 'If anyone religious comes round knocking on my door and disturbing me this Christmas, I'll tell them I'm a Satanist and I can't stop because I've got a goat on the stove,' he growled, probably being serious.

One of the things Paul could finally stop worrying about that winter was money. The amount of cash you can earn on tour in regional theatres is one of the big secrets of the entertainment industry. People constantly mock how former stars are believed to have hit rock bottom by playing in various seaside resorts rather than appearing on national television. But as Paul was finding out, those live gigs can be incredibly lucrative, especially if you could sell enough merchandise in the intervals. When pressed, Paul tried to be evasive about the financial rewards he had made. 'Lily's bought me a shower. After forty years of tipping a pan of water over my head that's pretty good,' he joked.

In reality, though, Lily had paid for a whole lot more. Paul had finally moved from his council flat to a flash pad near the famous Le Pont de la Tour restaurant beside London's Tower Bridge. He had set up his own independent production company, Wildflower, with Brendan. And he was mixing in some extraordinary circles. When Cher appeared on the *Big Breakfast* bed, for example, the pair got on so well that they swapped numbers and met up again for drinks shortly afterwards – at the time Cher was living just across the Thames from Paul in Wapping. The following spring Paul took Lily over to LA to report on the Oscars for the *Big Breakfast* – and found that Cher could lead him even deeper into the entertainment A-list. One afternoon he and Ian McKellen were on their way back from seeing David Hockney when they met up with Cher in her extraordinary Malibu beach house. 'If you have to smoke, go out to the beach,' he remembers her telling him with a smile, before dragging him round to Goldie Hawn's house for tea. It was heady stuff for the boy from Birkenhead who had thought the biggest star he would ever meet would be Cleo Laine.

Later that year, Paul's love of travel and love of the celebrity lifestyle came together again when he was invited to spend a few days at Elton John's home in Nice. But this time the stick-thin Paul wasn't entirely comfortable. 'There were these Versace models in T-bag underpants, just like visions. And I got there and thought: "There's no bloody way I'm lying on a sunbed in me shorts, looking like I've just come off *Tenko*, the colour of milk and a mass of freckles on my back," so I nearly turned heel and came right home.' Fortunately, Paul had an ally – Elton himself. 'He wouldn't strip off either so we sat there in the shade like two little maiden aunts. Sad but true.'

Living it large chez Cher, Goldie or Elton were some of the many huge perks of Paul's new life. He wasn't going to apologise for enjoying every minute of them – and he was thrilled that they gave him a whole new subject to rant about in interviews. 'I'm not going to be one of those stars who say, "I'm ever so humble and I love a cup of tea."' He would say to journalists, tongue only half in his cheek. 'I don't like tea. I like getting slaughtered, thank you very much. I love five-star treatment. I love fame and flash living because I've had poverty. I've lived through that and you can stick it. I don't want to go back to the Northern cobbles.' And he had no tolerance for those who said they wouldn't mind if it all ended tomorrow. 'I say that if it all ended tomorrow I would be one of the most evil, bitter and twisted people around. I'd be the one sitting in front of the telly saying: "He's crap. That's rubbish." I'd be writing letters to *Points of View* under assumed names. I'll never go quietly. I don't want all this to end because I'm having far too much of a good time. And I love spending money.'

Those that knew Paul best in the late 1990s could attest that most of these claims were simply exaggerations to help give reporters something to write about. Yes, of course he loved the good life. But Paul O'Grady himself hadn't really changed. And he could go back to his old life in an instant if he ever needed to. Big sister Shelagh still chatted away to him on the phone twice a week and hit the town with him on her rare trips to London. She said fame hadn't changed him at all. 'He's always just the same old Paul. If he walked into our house now he would just light up a fag and put the kettle on.' *Sun* reporter Garry Bushell, who had now known Paul for years, put it differently. 'He's still common as muck,' he joked after visiting Paul's posh new home and hearing stories about his new celebrity friends.

As proof that he had achieved more credible success he was soon to be offered his first major advertising campaign – a £150,000 promotion for the Ford Escort. Three things attracted Paul to the job. First came the money. Second was the humour in the adverts – a series that would take the mickey out of some recent Levis ads. And thirdly, Paul liked the fact that the campaign wasn't just for Lily. He would get to show his face in it as well. In the original Levis ads a six-foot half-Filipino, half-

Chinese transvestite had been shaving in the back of a cab. In the Ford campaign Paul is seen as himself in the back of the Escort – though it is Lily who climbs out of the car to pose for photographers at a West End première. The transformation is shown in some quick-fire flashbacks before Lily says: 'I change my genes in mine'. It loses a little in translation on the page, but the commercial was fun to make and would plant a tiny seed in the back of Paul's mind. Could I ever make it on screen in my own right? Or will I always need to have Lily waiting in the wings to dazzle the crowds?

Before he thought any more about it, Paul was to meet the biggest and most dazzling celebrity of all – and the one he had thought he respected the least. It was Princess Diana and the event reminded Paul, of all people, that you should never judge a book by its cover. The meeting was in fact a totally private affair. It had nothing to do with Paul's fame and wasn't recorded by any cameras. It took place when Paul was visiting a friend – one of far too many of his friends – who was in a hospice dying of Aids.

At this time the full stigma of HIV and Aids had still to be fully broken and hope for the future remained in short supply. Paul's own life had been hard hit by the disease. When he had left Merseyside to live in London nearly a dozen of his gay friends were heading down south as well. By 1995 only Paul and a handful of the others remained. The rest had been claimed by Aids and at one point he says it felt like he was going to a funeral 'every other day'.

In the early days of the disease, when Paul had still been working for Camden Council, its impact on him was even harder. He sometimes felt he worked all day with battered mums throwing everything away on alcohol and heroin. Then he went home to try and comfort his sick and dying friends. They had been the toughest of times.

In the hospice, Paul and his pal had been chatting away as usual when they were told that Princess Diana was due to visit that afternoon and was hoping to talk to as many residents and their visitors as possible. Paul vowed not to be one of them. 'Right, that's me off. I can't stand that shower of parasites,' he said, standing up sharply and reaching for his coat. But his friend held him back.

'Look, I hate them as well. But you've got to stay here to support me.'

Paul looked at his mate in silence. He knew he couldn't abandon him to face the royal circus alone. But he thought back to all those days at home in Birkenhead when his dad had ripped pictures of the Queen out of the encyclopaedia and thrown them in the bin. The royals were parasites, he had been taught. Some thirty years later he still believed it and the last thing he wanted to do was to meet one of them. But at least he had a pretty strong idea that he wouldn't have to shake anyone's hand. He didn't think Diana would risk doing that in an Aids ward. She would be there for a couple of minutes, she would keep her distance, have some pictures taken and then she would swan off back to her palace, he decided. He despised her already.

All his life the one thing Paul has never shied from is admitting when he's been wrong. He is happy to admit that he was wrong about Diana. 'She was there for an hour, and honest to God she was a cracker,' he says, thinking back to how she had shaken as many hands as she could – how she had hugged patients, visitors and staff alike. How she had sat on the patients' beds and chatted away as if she didn't have a care in the world. 'With my pal she just sat down next to him and gabbed away like she had known him all her life. I couldn't believe how someone who came from her stock could be such an amazing, down to earth person. She was brilliant.'

The visit, one of the many Diana made to Aids charities in those confused and awful days, would end up making a huge difference to public perception of the disease. Until Diana started to sit on those beds and hold those hands there had still been a fear that you could catch Aids just from touching its victims. She alone had the courage to prove otherwise – and while Paul never forgot her, it turned out that she hadn't forgotten him either.

Two months later he had just given up his regular role on the *Big Breakfast* and had time to kill. Mooching around Harrods one day he felt a hand on his shoulder. It was Diana. 'She asked if I missed doing breakfast telly. She said the lads, William and Harry, loved me.' And Paul admits he was as starstruck as everyone else who met the late Princess. Though the feeling didn't extend to anyone else in her troubled family. 'Don't get me wrong, though, she's the only one of them I like. I can't stand the rest of them,' he told pals after coming clean about his conversion. So when news came through of Diana's death in the underpass in Paris on Sunday 31 August, 1997 he was as devastated as everyone else. So devastated, in fact, that he rose before dawn on the day of her funeral to stand silent and anonymous near Whitehall to watch the procession. Something in him responded to Diana's position as the interloper at the royal party, the inconvenient woman they had tried to freeze out and forget. The woman they had tried to pretend didn't exist because she offended their view of how wives – and ex-wives – should behave.

Paul happily reports that he whooped 'like a French Revolution peasant' at Lord Spencer's extraordinary funeral address. To prove that his opinions were more than skin deep Paul would ultimately opt out of that year's *Royal Variety Performance*. Still feeling raw about Diana's death, he thought it was too soon for royalty to be carrying on as if nothing had happened.

Free from the early morning routine of the *Big Breakfast*, Paul was ready for new challenges. He was also hugely proud of what he had achieved on the show, and of the steely discipline he had demonstrated by turning up every morning and never once letting down his guard. 'I was the only one on the *Big Breakfast* who never swore on air,' he says. 'I behaved myself when I was on *Richard & Judy*, too, because I know how far to go. I've always known that I've got three audiences: Lily on tour when I can be as rude as I like, Lily on late-night telly where I've got to cool it a bit, and mainstream Lily where I can't swear.' As high-wire acts go it wasn't always easy to stay balanced – but with Paul's comedy rival Julian Clary only just reappearing on television some five years after his too-blue comments about Norman Lamont at the British Comedy Awards, there was plenty of incentive to get it right.

In London, Paul was continuing to make good friends. He spent a lot of time hanging out at the relatively anonymous Gerry's Bar on Soho's Dean Street, the old haunt of Keith Waterhouse and Jeffrey Bernard. Paul was soon thick as thieves with the bar's Irish landlord and got offered a rare honorary membership, which he treasures to this day.

But Paul was also surprising friends and fans alike by escaping London whenever he got the chance. His favourite hideaway was in the Hebrides where he first found a perfect bed and breakfast on the edge of the white beaches of Barra. After several visits he then found somewhere even further off the beaten track – a tiny cottage with no phone, no television and just one electric socket. Paul listened to the shipping forecast on Radio 4 and the news on the World Service. He took long walks in all weathers. And he slept for hour after wonderful hour. With nothing to do and no distractions he would sometimes go back to bed in the middle of the afternoon, to recharge his batteries in preparation for the other part of his life back in London.

'I get serious longings for the island, absolute cravings

when I'm not there,' says the man who most fans would have thought would jet off to New York or the Caribbean in his spare time. 'You can't beat a lock-in in the local pub and a yak with the fishermen. The best bit is I don't think any of them have a clue who I am.' What might also surprise people is that the worse the weather, the more Paul likes his trips to the Hebrides. One of his favourite visits was when massive storms and horizontal rains left him stuck there for five days. He jokes that he hopes for the same weather and the same enforced extended stay on every subsequent visit. The long empty days on Barra clear his head and help him put his wild new life in perspective. 'Showbusiness can burn you up. The smallest irritations can turn into mega problems. If I have to wait ten minutes for a bus then I go crackers. But I can sit on a rock and stare out to sea and, bang, all my worries disappear. I have no make-up, no costumes, no props to worry about up there. I can just be little boring old me.'

Back in London, the first thing that greeted Paul was an unexpected rejection. He was told that the production team for the Saturday night *National Lottery* show had apparently rejected him as a regular presenter because they thought he wasn't a 'suitable family entertainer'. 'Me – who's done *Richard & Judy*!' he said, only half joking, when Garry Bushell quizzed him about the snub. 'Apparently I'm "too camp", which must make Dale Winton Jean-Claude Van Damme.' Warming to his theme and happy to joke about his career being over, Paul carried on spinning stories. 'I've said for years that there is no way I would do panto but I'll probably need to now. I'll end up at the end of some grotty pier playing Dame Trot. Or I'll be sitting at home with a bottle of cider saying, "I used to be big, it's the pubs that got small". Not a suitable family entertainer indeed!'

What helped Paul make light of this rare rejection was the fact that his career very clearly wasn't over. In fact, a different section of the BBC had just given the green light for his biggest prime-time show so far. *The Lily Savage Show*, the name he had given to his racy live act for the past two years, was about to arrive on Sunday night television for a lucrative six-week run. 'It's going to be good old fashioned family entertainment – if your family happens to be the Mansons,' he joked as the news broke.

But putting the series together would bring a new set of ups and downs for Paul and everyone around him. At first the news was good. The show was beginning just as newspaper investigations were revealing the ridiculous demands some diva-like celebrities were making before they would appear on a film set or even a chat show. Paul laughed at them like everyone else and said he was happy to reveal there were no such 'riders' on his own contracts. 'Why would I want M&Ms with all the brown ones taken out? Do me a favour. After ten years as a social worker, I know that some people have hideous lives and don't complain about them, so I won't start moaning about things like the colour of my car to work or my hotel rooms on tour,' he said.

So everyone at the BBC probably relaxed, expecting to work with a cross between Mother Theresa and Nelson Mandela. They were in for a nasty shock, as Paul himself is happy to admit. A team of writers had been put together to help write the sketches but Paul suddenly felt there was no way he could let Lily go and trust her fate to anyone else. No one knew Lily like him, he said. No one else could be true to her. And truth had always been her greatest strength.

'The minute the show's pre-production started I turned into a complete total raving lunatic,' he admits ruefully. 'I was a nightmare. A monster everyone was scared of. You should have seen the faces of the writers. Just up from Cambridge after two jobs and I was binning their scripts,' he says. And binning those first few scripts was only the start. After some tense meetings in the production offices Paul took even more drastic action. 'In the end I sacked the lot of them on the spot and wrote it all myself in a couple of weeks.'

The rush and the panic meant the whole show would all be a bit hit and miss – and explains why Paul reckons he very nearly had a nervous breakdown as the deadlines loomed and the pressure built up. He admits he had panic attacks, felt manic and demented and worried that he was cracking up. The big time was not as easy as he had hoped. 'No wonder half the people in this business go potty or get into booze or drugs,' he said of the new high stress, high stakes world of mainstream national television.

As he sat at home working on scripts until the early

hours, Paul came up with a massive dream list of guest stars. He had written a series of sketch ideas for old favourites like *Coronation Street*'s Liz Dawn as well as Cher, Helen Mirren, Michael Ball, Des Lynam and Carol Vorderman. Not surprisingly, several of the stars weren't going to be available at such short notice so Paul was often back at square one the following night, after a fruitless day hitting the phones trying to round up replacement acts.

To make matters worse, filming the show would also prove a challenge. Paul had learned his trade performing live and had been free to say whatever he wanted on the *Big Breakfast*. Sticking to a script where every pause for laughs was timed down to the second was a nightmare. Everything took longer to film than he had thought it would and the lack of spontaneity was a real problem for him. As was the lack of feedback from an audience who sometimes had to sit through the same sketch half a dozen times while the producers ironed out some hard-to-spot problem. 'As if all that's not bad enough, when I'm on autocue I look like I'm going to have a stroke. I'm never doing telly again, I'm going back on tour,' he said to himself every night after leaving the recordings. What added to the pressure was that expectations were high. 'Word has it that O'Grady has mellowed for his first major TV series,' Garry Bushell wrote in the *Sun* just before transmission. 'Yeah – and look, there's Pinky and Perky piloting a Virgin airbus.'

So would *The Lily Savage Show* be a hit? Looking

back there were plenty of classic Lily lines – many of them very close to the bone for a Sunday night slot on the Beeb. One of Paul's favourite quick-fire lines came when one of the most important guests, BBC1 Controller Alan Yentob, said he wanted to paint Lily.

'Will you sit for me, for a small fee?' Alan asked.

'For fifty pounds I'll lay down for you, love,' she replied, as the audience roared.

Fortunately, the guest list that Paul had managed to pull together was as strong as his best jokes. Paul had got the likes of Anthea Turner, Stephanie Beacham and Elton John to join him, and even had Janet Street-Porter playing the role of his much put-upon floor manager. Sonia was back in the act, reprising her stage role as Vera's daughter Bunty, while Daniel Newman was there to play Jason, and everyone was left wondering if the elusive Vera might make a rare public appearance. As usual Lily's name-dropping made for some good jokes. In a spoof interview with *Hello!* magazine Lily showed readers around her glamorous home at 63 Upitself Avenue. 'Richard and July live over there and Katie Boyle lives next door. So it's a bit of a rough neighbourhood,' she declared.

A final memorable moment came courtesy of Jason Connery, the heart-throb son of 007 star Sean. He and Paul had met up in Edinburgh during the summer's festival and Jason had said he would happily play Lily's husband in a sketch. They also shared a lengthy on-screen kiss. 'That scene took three takes to get right but

I don't think Lily was complaining. She enjoyed every minute,' Paul joked afterwards. The critics, though, were not so enthusiastic. *The Lily Savage Show* never really did set the world on fire and Paul was deflated when the six-week run came to an end.

'When I met him then he was very grey-haired and very grey-faced,' remembers *Daily Mirror* writer Brian Reade. 'He said he was exhausted.' But he was also determined to learn from the experience. 'Some of it was very good,' Paul told himself. Faint praise perhaps, but enough to see him through the negative reviews. The problem had been in the preparation. Not having enough time and taking too much on himself had stretched Lily too thinly over the show's run. Fortunately, both issues could be put right for a future show. And in the meantime, Paul found that he could still earn some comedy kudos and make some extra money. Television had a new waste-not-want-not attitude and the out-takes and racier scenes from the show were pulled together and released on video as *The Untransmittable Lily Savage Show*. Paul got the last laugh, as usual – this time all the way to the bank.

Best news of all was that Lily had gone and won herself a big new job while everyone was focusing on the Sunday night show. It was only for a one-off. But it could – and indeed did – lead on to much more. The BBC was planning to bring back *Blankety Blank* as a Christmas special. They thought Lily was the ideal new presenter to shake off the ghosts of Terry Wogan and Les

Dawson. Paul couldn't have agreed more. He never for a moment felt that he was selling out or dumbing down by taking on such a cheesy old show. In truth it was the cheesy nature and the ancient history that appealed to him. He also felt it offered Lily a superb structure in which to shine. The framework was perfect for her – plenty of banter with the contestants and the celebrities, plenty of chance for arch comments and growling asides. 'It's ideal for me because you're supposed to be insulting. I told them I want it to be exactly the way it was with Les Dawson. No fancy prizes and the same corny guests. I just can't wait to do it,' Paul said, as the plans were firmed up. The experts seemed to agree. '*Blankety Blank* is a gameshow that relies solely on the banter between the host and the celebrity panel,' said TV critic Vicky Spavin. 'So Lily is the perfect host.'

He was still feeling good about it all when filming began. 'Look at this set. I asked for something evocative of Rome and they gave me something that looks like Brent Cross shopping centre,' he snarled, while jokingly threatening to walk out. What was giving Paul his new-found confidence that autumn was the fact that he really did think he had learned from the problems on *The Lily Savage Show*.

Once more, the *Blankety Blank* producers had presented him with scripts, gags and links written by a host of other writers. Once more, Paul had rejected almost all of them in favour of finding Lily's words on his own. This time though he had given himself more time. He had also told the slightly nervous producers that Lily would ad lib and go off message whenever she felt like it. This was the edge that had turned her into such a powerful live performer. It was what viewers missed when she was forced to stick to a pre-agreed script. Freedom of expression would bring her alive on *Blankety Blank*. The more relaxed Paul was when he hit any stage as Lily, the better her act would be. At the end of 1997, when he got ready for the pilot epsisode of *Blankety Blank*, he was more relaxed than he had been in years. It would show through. It would ensure he ended the year with what looked like it could be the biggest hit of his career.

Audiences seemed to have loved seeing *Blankety Blank* back on screen with its larger than life and mouthy new hostess. So a full series was commissioned. Lily was going to become even bigger, and more famous than ever – and the brilliant thing for Paul was that he could get all of the benefits of fame and fortune with very few of the downsides.

When she was in costume Lily was one of the most recognisable women in Britain. But Paul was one of the most anonymous of men – and for the moment this suited him just fine. When he went out for a few drinks with his friends in the soaps he was always reminded of just how high the price of fame could be. 'It was impossible for them to walk down the street or go out for a meal. I knew I just couldn't handle being that famous,' he said. So while the paparazzi snapped away at his famous friends, Paul himself walked alongside them unnoticed. Reporters who interviewed Paul said that if you looked at him and were asked to guess what he did for a living, you would think of nothing racier than a graphic designer or an architect. 'You might think he was a bank manager, until he opened his mouth when his rasping voice might give it away,' said one.

What Paul thrived on was the fact that no one really wanted to know about Mr Paul O'Grady any more. They just wanted to know about Lily Savage. They wanted her opinions, her thoughts, her feelings. It was the ultimate proof that Paul had created what people saw as a living, breathing entity. That he really had given her life.

The only annoyance was that when he was mentioned as Lily's creator he was so often described as a drag queen – which he found lazy, discriminatory journalism. 'Barry Humphries is never called a drag act because he's a heterosexual male. But I'm called one because I'm a gay man. It's homophobic and it's wrong as there is nothing remotely sexual about what I do. I dress up as a woman for financial purposes, nothing else.'

And the money was really starting to roll in. As the full series of *Blankety Blank* was about to be launched Paul signed two huge new advertising campaigns. One was for Pretty Polly tights and would focus on his extraordinary legs – ironic, because as a man they were the one part of him he always tried to keep covered up. 'I look like I had rickets as a child. In shorts I look like two Woodbines hanging out of the packet,' he said, repeating the old story of how he had sat fully dressed in the shade at Elton John's house in the south of France. But take on Lily's persona, pull on tights and a pair of high heels and it's a different story. 'Lily has legs to die for; they seem never ending,' Carol Smillie said after appearing on *The Lily Savage Show*. Pretty Polly agreed. They gave him his biggest pay packet to date for a massive poster, newspaper and television campaign – and Paul loved stoking the false rumours that he had turned into the new Betty Grable by spending £3,000 a month insuring his legs for £500,000 each.

The next big pay cheque came when he agreed to be the new national face of Bingo in a £5 million advertising campaign. It was a far cry from Paul's early days as a performer, when he had needed to swallow his pride to become the voice of both Blu Loo toilet cleaners and a cat litter tray in his first couple of commercials. By the time his big new adverts hit the screens, Lily was appearing in her new weekly BBC slot on *Blankety Blank*. She was also being asked to be a guest on almost every chat show going; she always gave superb value and normally overshadowed her host. But Paul was always there with a laugh to keep her feet on the ground. 'You're in the entertainment A-list. Are you finally ready to conquer Hollywood?' Lily was asked.

'Hollywood? Hollyhead, more like,' she said dismissively.

That said, Paul was well aware of the power of celebrity and television – which led him into some of the other anecdotes he loved to recount on the chat show circuit. 'I've rung up people like the gas board and said, "I'm the producer of *Watchdog*. If the engineer's not round here in ten minutes then tonight, on the programme, you're going to be the main subject." They were round in a shot. Then I've phoned up the bank and said, "Where's my Switch card? I've waited two weeks. Right, you're on *Richard & Judy* in the morning." The power of *Richard & Judy*. It gets things done,' he joked. On other chat show sofas he would have Lily speak out on one of his other obsessions – how the soaps were losing their way. *Coronation Street* was going through a *Neighbours*-style phase of introducing an endless series of young and beautiful characters. Paul hated it. 'The *Street* shouldn't be about image; it should be about the Elsie Tanner, middle-aged, past-their-sell-by-date women, fighting and surviving,' he said.

Funnily enough, *Coronation Street* seemed to be the only show Paul could watch at that time without seeing Lily pop up in some cameo role. 'Every time I turned the telly on I saw her – even the *South Bank Show* wasn't safe,' he said, after she popped up on that in a clip with her old pal Lesley Garrett. The *Blankety Blank*s were all filmed in a matter of weeks but seemed to last a lifetime when they were finally shown. If it wasn't quite overkill, Paul at least feared he might be over-cooking his golden goose.

'I knew I just had to get off the box. I also needed to hear the sound of a live audience again. Telly is like working in an office. You go in, you do it and you go home. You might just as well be talking to yourself. Live theatres keep you alive because the audience are so part of the show and they're different every night.' So Paul signed up for yet another gruelling series of tours – where he would immediately start making headlines.

The first bizarre story broke in Edinburgh where Paul was back at the Festival alongside Jo Brand and Julian Clary. The bad old days when he and Brendan had slept on mates' floors out in the suburbs were long gone, however. This year, Paul was booked into the five-star Caledonian hotel right on Princes Street. But old habits die hard, so he was partying as much as ever – and he nearly caused a major incident in the early hours of one morning when he got lost in the hotel's many long corridors. Feeling a little tired, Paul had his high heels in one hand and a cigarette in the other as he shuffled towards what he thought was his room. But he was on the wrong floor. Triggering a full-scale security alert, it turned out he was about to try and open the bedroom door where one Tony Blair was staying en route to his summer stay at Balmoral. The new Prime Minister's protection officers say they have faced many threats over the years. But none quite as exotic-looking as Paul, who was gently but firmly led back to his room just before dawn.

Edinburgh had been the warm-up act for the real business of the tour. The opening night was in Bournemouth before the show criss-crossed the country and ended in Paul's home town, at the Liverpool Empire, eight weeks later. 'A word of warning: Lily is much more blue live than on telly,' the *Independent* warned in its preview. But that seemed to be what everyone was hoping for. Box offices at all fourteen venues said the phones started ringing as soon as the dates were unveiled. Paul was once again going to hear the three little words he cherished so much: 'Standing room only'.

The live shows had been a real tonic. Lily's act was sharper and sometimes harsher than ever. So Paul was on a roll. His old pal Barbara Windsor persuaded him to join her on a celebrity Christmas edition of *Ready, Steady, Cook.* The show was filmed in late November in the BBC's studios in White City and the crew said it was one of the most manic they had ever worked on. After the recording Paul and Barbara spent long hours talking back stage. One of the many things about Barbara, which Paul had never denied, was how many times she had reinvented herself and how diverse her professional career had been. He wanted her advice on the next big challenge he had taken on. He had agreed to go back on the West End stage in another full-length musical. Barbara said she knew he would be a sensation. But by the time he got to the rehearsal rooms Paul wasn't so sure.

'Forget it. My feet are both marked with big "Ls". You would have more luck getting me to learn quantum physics in two days than learning those dances,' Paul told his new show's producers. He was going to play Mrs Hannigan in *Annie* and had just watched a run-through of the big dance routine that would mark one of his first scenes. *Birds of a Feather* star Lesley Joseph had been performing the routine since the show had opened at the Victoria Palace Theatre in the autumn. But could Paul master it in time to take over from her at the end of the year? He thought back to everything Barbara Windsor had told him. She had knuckled down, retrained and learned new skills whenever she had needed to. So he swore that he would do the same. He gave the dance steps everything he had, and within two weeks the producers and director were giving him a standing ovation in rehearsals. Not quite so successful, everyone admitted, was his mastery of the American accent the role demanded. 'I might keep the voice up for the first night, just for the critics to say it's appalling, and then go back to the Liverpool accent,' he joked.

In most respects, though, the Scouse drawl was what the production team and the audiences wanted. 'To be honest the way we decided to do it from was the start was to have Lily Savage playing the part,' remembers director Martin Charnin. And he thought she was so strong that there was no knowing where this sort of role-play might end. Martin was convinced that one day Paul could be Lily playing Liz Taylor's role of Martha in *Who's Afraid of Virginia Woolf?* 'Everyone thinks that's a wonderful – if complicated – idea,' he said with a smile.

But before this could even be considered there was the small matter of Paul's first night on 15 December to worry about. And fortunately everything went like a dream. Mo Mowlam and a crowd of Paul's old pals were in the stalls to show their support and he turned in a blinding performance. The producers immediately offered him an extension on his original two-month commitment to the show.

Hoofing it up in a classic musical was a real dream come true for Paul, and he was surprised how much he enjoyed playing someone rather than Lily – though the similarities between her and Mrs Hannigan were never lost on the audiences. What he also loved was the fact that doing six evening shows and two matinees a week meant Christmas was severely disrupted again – just the way he liked it. 'I hate Christmas, I always will,' he likes to proclaim, only half joking. 'Let's face it, Christmas is all about being stuck in Brent Cross shopping centre where there's *Here It Is, Merry Christmas* on a loop tape. And the people on the counter are verging on the psychopathic because they've had to listen to it all day for weeks on end. And there are all those people going around shouting: "Aaagh, I haven't got me brandy butter. What am I going to do?"'

At chez Savage things weren't much better apparently. Paul reckoned he was the only one of his friends who could even begin to cook a big dinner, so he was the one facing all the pressure. 'I'm in the kitchen sweating like a glassblower's bum, making this dinner that everyone's too pissed to eat and doesn't want to anyway, and you sit watching crap telly and I just wish: "Get me to New Year's Eve when I can get slaughtered out of my mind."'

In 1998, though, Christmas wasn't all bad for Paul.

He bought one of his very first lottery tickets that month – and instantly won £1,000, which he spent taking all the little girls from the show out for a wonderful day's shopping in London. And almost everywhere they went they saw Lily's face staring back at them. Life-size posters promoting the latest recording of her live shows were in most of the shop windows while all her previous videos still seemed to be on every shelf. Then there was her first book, a sort of A–Z thing, which was billed as the ultimate guide to: 'Life, the universe and shoplifting'. As agony aunts go, Lily was on top form. Shirley Conran, the original domestic superwoman, had famously said back in 1975 that life was 'too short to stuff a mushroom'. Two decades on Lily felt that it was too short even to cook oven chips. 'Just open a tin instead,' she advised harassed housewives, before launching into other chapters explaining everything from how to poison your husband to how to get rid of dodgy stains on your duvet.

As the sales figures came in, the merchandising men said the stick-thin Lily could well be worth more than her weight in gold. Paul was estimated to have broken the million-pound mark in career earnings that Christmas – not bad for an act which had begun life collecting just £40 a night in cash at some of the capital's roughest pubs. But not every promotional opportunity came off – the prototype Lily doll, which came with a little bottle of booze and a cigarette, was put on hold. 'WH Smith said we couldn't have a fag in it,' Paul said with a smile. 'But she's known to be an alcoholic, shoplifting prostitute. She's Lily Savage, not Maria von Trapp.'

Cleverly, though, the Lily Savage that Paul was showing to the public was very different to the one the pubs and clubs crowd had seen in the late 1980s. He says he has always hated it when rich and successful comics talk down to their audiences by making out they still go to launderettes or struggle to make ends meet. 'There has to be truth in comedy. If there isn't, it won't work. Audiences see through you if you try to pretend you are something you're not,' he says. So now it was obvious that he was doing very nicely he felt he had to reflect that in Lily. It meant that routines about her fiddling her electricity meter or stealing from the supermarket were out. Instead, he hinted at some 'costa del crime' style windfall and moved her into a vast mansion in Hampstead where she horrified the neighbours.

'It's tasteless, very *Spend, Spend, Spend*,' he said of the home he conjured up. And he loved recreating other parts of her story. When the latest Lily went shoplifting, she would do it on Bond Street, for example. It made the act seem fresh and it seemed to fit in perfectly with the new Posh and Becks culture.

However good his new act was going to be for Lily, Paul knew it would be a while before many of his fans saw it. *Annie* was ending its run in London and Paul had signed up to go on the road with the show that spring. He loved it because it gave him a chance to spend more time with different sets of friends across the country. In

Manchester, where *Annie* was booked into the Opera House, Paul got to hang out at The Old Grapes. Liz Dawn from *Coronation Street* was one of the bar's owners and had long since become a good friend. So late at night after taking his bows at the Opera House and wiping off all his stage make-up, Paul headed to the Grapes for some downtime. 'It's the sort of place where you can hang out with coppers consuming gallons of cider and eating scampi and chips,' he remembers. 'It was just a great place to be.'

When he was on tour Paul had similar favourites in most other towns and cities – bars and restaurants where he often knew the owners and the regulars well and was welcomed back as an old friend. Contrary to expectations, he says he never wants to be in a city's 'in place' just for the sake of it. In London, for example, he still loved the Atlantic Bar because of the big soft sofas he could relax on. 'When I say I want to go there for a drink people tell me it's not hip any more, but then I'm not a hip person. I go places because I feel comfortable there, not for any other reason,' he says.

When his run in *Annie* was finally over, Paul was ready to live it up once more. In his first few days off he flew over to Dublin where he threw himself into what felt like a permanent party. Evenings began with a big bowl of Irish stew with six fresh oysters on the side. Then there would be cold real Guinness, the kind he swears you can never quite replicate anywhere else in the world. After the pubs came the clubs – Lily's Bordello or the Pod being favourites. And all the while he knew that a good Dublin breakfast on Grafton Street would help him get started the following morning. Back in London shortly afterwards, he describes 'one glorious bender' when he went out on a Friday night and didn't come home till the following Wednesday. Not every moment of the five days has ever been fully accounted for.

But for all this rock-star style of excess the other, calmer side of Paul did frequently resurface. Whenever he needed a break, he still tried to get up to the Scottish islands for some fresh air, long walks and quiet nights. He found himself dreaming about the farms he had stayed on when in Ireland as a boy. Living so close to the centre of London was fantastic. But every now and then he felt he needed more space. 'I'm getting old,' he joked with his friends. 'I think I want to retire to the country.' What no one realised was that he was serious.

CHAPTER SEVEN
Country Life

Paul stood outside the farmhouse and gazed out across the Weald of Kent. The view was stunning – gentle hills, wide fields, dense woods and hardly another building to be seen. He had driven through the picture-postcard village of Aldington, and past several perfectly preserved Kentish oast houses to get to this particular farmhouse, and he felt immediately that he wanted to own it.

It was a perfect July day, the sun was strong and Paul couldn't hear anything but birdsong and a light rustle from the trees. There was no traffic noise, no sirens, none of the sounds that had surrounded him in Birkenhead and followed him to London. Yes, he thought, this six-bedroom farm really could be his retreat. It could be his home. He turned around and walked back into the hallway. The vast open-plan kitchen stretched out in front of him and he could imagine it filled with friends and laughter. There was a swimming pool in the more formal part of the grounds and beyond the cultivated gardens were nearly 200 acres of wide-open fields. I can have animals. I can be a farmer, Paul thought. It will be like stepping back in time to those wonderful days in Galway. This could be perfect.

But should he really buy it? As usual two very different voices in Paul's head were straining to be heard. The loudest was urging caution. It was the voice that had kept him in his council flat for so long, even after the money from Lily Savage had dwarfed his old social services salary. It was the voice that echoed so many of the attitudes he had learned as a child. The fear of debt, the worry that the wolf might once again appear at the door if things went wrong. The fear that he might end up back in Vicky Mansions if he blew everything and didn't care enough about tomorrow.

The other voice was telling him to throw caution to the wind and to live for today. This was the voice that had taken him to Manila as a teenager. The one that had persuaded him to step on to that stage as compère at the Elephant & Castle pub so long ago. It was the same voice that made him such great company and such a fun friend.

'I want it.' The second voice had won. Spending £650,000 on a place in the country was a huge step in 1999, when the average house price was still under

£85,000. But Paul could hardly say he hadn't earned it. Nor, given his endless workload, did he feel he didn't deserve it. What made the purchase a little more fun was the identity of the seller: Vic Reeves. In typical fashion, Paul didn't miss any opportunity to have a laugh at the comedian's expense when he was asked about his new home. 'Vic's left nothing behind. Lightbulbs, floorboards, the roof. He took the lot,' Paul joked with pals, after moving in at the end of August.

Paul's big challenge in those first weeks in Kent was finding enough furniture. Ten families in Birkenhead live in fewer rooms, he joked, and he had never expected to own such a big home himself. When he had spare days he loved heading out to local antique shops to browse around for pieces of art nouveau furniture – a style he had always loved and was finally learning more about. Outside the main house the grounds would soon be alive with animals. Pigs, cows and even horses would come later. He started with geese, immediately nicknamed the geestapo after they proved to be tougher and more frightening than most guard dogs. His first pair, which he called the Krays, actually had to be given away when they became too vicious to let any visitors come close to the house. The Fuhrer and Eva Braun, who replaced them, were only marginally less territorial.

The only problem Paul had with the house was a feeling that he couldn't spend enough time there. For Lily was still in demand. And Paul had plenty of other projects on the go – some of which would shock friends and fans alike. His friends were first to raise their eyebrows when the fiercely anti-royal Paul agreed to attend a big function with the Duke of Edinburgh at St James's Palace. Two key reasons persuaded Paul to agree to the arrangement. First, he approved of the charity it was supporting – the Duke's long-standing awards scheme for young people. The scheme members had been asked which stars they most admired and who they would like to present them with their awards. Lily had topped their poll, hence her surprise invitation.

The second reason Paul accepted the invitation was that the courtiers told him he would be the first person to ever attend a royal presentation at the palace in drag. If you want to be famous for something, be famous for that, he told pals. And he didn't regret it for a second – he won a huge ovation when Lily tottered over to the front of the stage to hand out the certificates. 'Prince Philip turned to me and said: "My goodness, you're popular." I think he thought I was Princess Margaret,' Paul joked afterwards, though he says the republican in him wasn't quashed by the occasion.

That said, Paul could hardly deny that he was starting to live in royal style himself. He was back in panto that Christmas, and in a burst of rare showbusiness extravagance he hired a helicopter to get him from his Birmingham theatre back to Kent on Christmas Eve. But in true Lily fashion even this ended in farce – he jumped out of the passenger seat and stepped right into a cowpat in his own front field.

Seven days later, on a raucous New Year's Eve, Paul followed his dream of seeing his new home full of friends – between them they drank what seemed like enough champagne to fill a small lake, and corks would continue to be found both inside and outside his house for the next three months. Putting down roots in the country had turned out to be a brilliant idea and it was from his farm that he planned his next big career coup. ITV were offering him big money to jump channels yet again – and this time they wanted him to take *Blankety Blank* with him. After little more than two-dozen Saturday-night shows, Paul had started to win up to nine million viewers for the Beeb, a rare ratings success among a sea of flops.

The BBC was desperate not to lose their sole prime-time ratings winner. But a quirk in the way the latest contracts had been written meant that it didn't have much choice. The actual rights to *Blankety Blank* were owned by the Australian production company Grundy, not the Beeb. So if Grundy wanted to offer it to a higher bidder when each contract expired then it was free to do so. When Paul said he was happy to do the switch, the company set it all in motion. *Blankety Blank*, synonymous with BBC1 for more than 30 years, would have a new home by the autumn. Or would it?

'Oh my God. It's John Birt.'

Paul was at home in Kent when the call came through on his mobile. It was the Director General of the BBC, making a personal plea for Paul to stay with the channel.

Blankety Blank belonged there, he said. The show's heritage, from Terry Wogan to Les Dawson, gave it roots on the channel. And if Paul changed his mind they could come up with any number of other shows for him to consider as well. Des Lynam and Ross Kemp had both just defected to ITV. Birt was desperate to stop Paul from following suit. But after a tense conversation Paul knew he couldn't agree to stay. For a start, ITV was in the process of putting together an incredible two-year deal worth some £1 million. And its plans for both *Blankety Blank* and a set of other shows that would carry Paul or Lily's name seemed a lot more concrete and exciting. 'I'm sorry, John,' Paul said when he made up his mind. He was leaving the BBC politely and on good terms. But he was leaving.

On a lighter note, he said he had very specific plans for how he wanted *Blankety Blank* to be when it reached its new home. 'I know it's almost impossible but we are going to go even cheaper on the prizes,' he joked with reporters. 'Forget *Who Wants To Be A Trillionaire* or whatever it's called. We're going for book tokens, cans of pale ale, Party Sevens and a Teasmade. And that's only if you win three weeks in a row. It's how British gameshows should be.' The big gamble for everyone concerned was whether a star and a show could survive such a dramatic channel hop – questions were already being asked, for example, about whether *Blankety Blank* had enough drama to cope with a commercial break, or whether it would get buried in ITV's far more successful stable of shows. Had it only done well on the BBC because there was so little competition?

At first it seemed as if the show was a perfect fit in its new home. Lily was able to get away with being a lot more risqué than her former bosses had allowed and the initial reviewers seemed to approve. A year's worth of shows were filmed in quick succession and while some of the top prizes did end up sounding pretty good – holidays rather than Teasmades, for example – Paul was initially pleased with the move. He was also working overtime again, adding a new series of *Lily Live!* for ITV to the list of his other commitments. The first six episodes, broadcast on Saturday nights, would be followed up by a second series the following autumn.

But while the ratings were healthy, some of Paul's friends were starting to wonder if he was losing his touch. 'Lily was wasted on *Blankety Blank* and spread too thinly on *Lily Live!*,' argued Garry Bushell, who now saw Paul as a friend as much as someone to write about in the *Sun*. Others were starting to take the same view. And Paul himself was starting to share everyone's doubts. He had been smearing on the mortician's wax, painting on his face, pulling on his wig and tights for nearly fifteen years. The high heels, the tight skirts, the hollow bras. It had paid off – in spades. But was it time to give it all up?

'I've made a monster and there are times when I have just got to get away from her,' he told friends, seriously worried that she was starting to take over his life. She had gone from a character he had brought to life for a few hours a night in the pub to being someone he was increasingly forced to be for more than ten hours a day. 'I love Lily, bless the dirty old bag. But what about me?' he asked. And what indeed?

After yet another gruelling day in the television studios, rehearsing for his latest tour, panto or personal appearance, Paul would come home and realise that he wasn't just fed up with dressing as Lily, he was sometimes fed up of her full stop. 'I come back to my flat some nights and there's an old leopardskin handbag on the floor and a pair of her shoes and some old coat. It's like living with some boozy old barmaid who's trashed the place. I think "Slag!" and start muttering about her under my breath.' It was a good joke and he trotted out comments like this all the time that autumn. But there was something serious to the talk as well – not least the fact that like so many of his fans Paul was starting to see Lily as a living and breathing entity. For so long he had enjoyed the anonymity of being in her shadow. But suddenly he felt like having a few days in the sun.

'When people talk about Lily they describe her as this glamour-puss star. When they talk about me they call me pasty-faced and go on about my cold sores.' Paul, amazingly, was feeling just a little bit jealous of his own comic creation – the dual life he had lived since childhood was starting to grate and he needed to do something about it.

'I felt like I was standing in the wings because it was

always Lily this and Lily that. People would talk about Lily like she was a separate entity and I didn't exist. It wasn't vanity but I would think, hang on a minute, it's me in the costume. Who do you think writes all this creature's things? Who makes her tick? Who winds her up? Me.'

Having said all this, Paul's problems weren't over on the rare occasions when he did stand in the limelight as himself. That summer he went to his first awards ceremony as plain old Paul O'Grady. And he hated it. Enjoying a stiff drink with friends the next day he told them he had felt like a nervous teenager, staring at the floor and trying to fade into the background. 'I wanted to have been wearing a wig and to have ten inches of slap to hide behind,' he said. When he talked to people as Lily at events like this he could say whatever outrageous thing came into his head and they would laugh. But when he tried to talk as Paul he felt paralysed. What if they don't like me? What if they just think I'm an idiot and go on to talk to someone more interesting?

Across the room at the awards show he had looked at other stars of the moment, such as Steve Coogan and Harry Enfield. They were naturally funny men who could hold their own in any company. But without Lily to hide behind Paul feared he had nothing to offer. He needed her, but he was terrified she was suffocating him. The double lives that he had started to live as a Birkenhead teenager were pulling at him once more. The old indecision over who he was and what he should do was making his life a misery. And this time he had an extra worry – about the passage of time. Paul was forty-four years old when he got back from the awards ceremony and wished he had been dressed as Lily. But just how much longer could he really keep on wearing high heels and hiding behind that act? He knew he didn't want to be 60, staggering around in a mini-skirt with a pot belly. He had never wanted to be Danny La Rue. So he decided he had to take action. He had spent his whole life rising to challenges and proving people wrong. Now he had found a new mountain to climb. He wanted to prove that he, Paul James O'Grady, was as funny and as popular as Lilian May Veronica Savage. He would learn not to look at the floor and avoid people's gaze. He would find a way to bring Lily's confidence into his own life. It wouldn't be easy. But then what of value in his life had been?

Of all things it was a 60-year-old shirt company from Wakefield that gave Paul the confidence to finally break out of Lily's shadow. The company, Double Two, was planning its first major advertising campaign in more than fifteen years and it had an estimated £500,000 to spend on poster sites, magazine and television ads. But the money wasn't what attracted Paul to the campaign. It was the message. The new slogan for Double Two was: When You Feel Like Fitting In. And the specific advertisement its agency had planned for Paul would show him as fans had rarely seen him before: as himself.

'The campaign plays off the expected double take of seeing famous people in less recognisable poses,' said Andrew Thomas of ad agency McCann-Erickson. Paul's pose was as the ultimate city gent. He looked sharp and smart in a blue striped shirt with a gold tie, his grey hair and glasses adding a sense of class to the Soho photographic studio where the first set of pictures was taken.

As a historical footnote, Paul felt a further affinity with Double Two as he chatted to the company's management that day. It seemed that back in the 1940s the company had been at the forefront of a very early switch of the sexes. The founders, Isaak Donner and Frank Myers, had originally wanted to make men's cotton shirts, Paul was told, but they were only able to find the kind of light artificial material that was used for women's blouses. Unsure of how to persuade that generation of men to get in touch with their feminine side, Isaak and Frank decided to turn things on their head. With the war effort gathering pace, it was the women working in munitions factories and on farms who needed to dress like men, not the other way around. So the company's first big sellers were traditional men's shirts that were re-styled for women. Sixty years later, a man who dressed as a woman would dress as a man to help carry the company into the next millennium. It was confusing, but there had to be some good karma there somewhere, Paul joked, after he was told about Double Two's heritage.

The other benefit of the job was the decent pay

cheque. And this was now very important to Paul. What only he and Brendan knew was that he was going to take a huge career gamble by pushing Lily back into the shadows. So Paul wanted plenty of extra money in the bank just in case it all went wrong. This desire for one more big payout spoke volumes about Paul's psyche. For money was the one thing his family background had taught him to treat with the utmost respect.

The attitude was illustrated when his mum had died just over a decade earlier and Paul had helped clear out her house with the rest of his extended family. He found a shoebox at the bottom of her wardrobe containing dozens of tiny half-crown life insurance policies dating back decades. The O'Grady clan's biggest fear was financial embarrassment – even after death. You could have holes in the shoes you wore at home when no one was looking. But there had to be good shoes put aside for best as well. There also had to be enough money put aside to pay for a decent funeral. It was a lesson Paul had always taken to heart. 'I've now got so many policies myself that I'd be worth an absolute fortune if I were to drop dead tomorrow,' he would joke. 'I'd be able to go off in style with a glass carriage and the Pope and seven dwarfs in attendance.'

More seriously, he vowed never to make the big mistakes of others in the entertainment world who thought the good times would last forever and forgot about the inevitable rainy days. Having had so little money for so long Paul was well aware of how wonderful it was to be in credit now. His accountant says Paul was always keen to be sure that enough money out of every pay cheque was put aside so his VAT and taxes could be paid when they fell due. People see me as a frivolous man, he sometimes told his advisers. But when it comes to business he was as serious as they come. 'If you suddenly start to earn big money later in life you can go either of two ways. You can spend, spend, spend. Or you can be sensible. I'm sensible,' he says. But with the new millennium underway and his finances in shape Paul was also ready to be a gambler.

He and Brendan had been talking about pitching a travel show to ITV for some time. But while everyone expected this to be a vehicle for Lily, the two of them had other ideas. Instead, Paul was going to go on a very personal journey – as himself. In the end it was the personal edge to the project that won over ITV's commissioning editors. There was a real point to the plan – Paul was going to retrace the steps he had taken when he had left Liverpool for the Far East more than twenty years earlier. He would revisit the places that had meant so much to him back then. And he would crack into those that had been denied to him as a near-penniless unknown. The pair got on a plane in the spring of 2000 and headed East. The latest adventure in Paul's high-wire career was about to begin.

CHAPTER EIGHT
Out in the Orient

The humidity hits you the moment you leave the air-conditioned splendour of the five-star Raffles Hotel in Singapore. But that hot spring day in 2000 Paul wasn't sweating only because of the heat. As he stepped out into the fierce early-morning sunshine he had hardly ever felt so exposed. The full implications of performing as himself were finally becoming clear. He could no longer hide behind the wig, the clothes, the fake fur, the fags and the make-up that had protected him for so long.

'Sorry guys, Lily is in a bin liner in my garage in Kent. She's screaming: "Let me out! Let me out!" But there's no one there to hear her,' he told the camera crew, trying to hide his fears with a joke as usual. But the crew didn't need reminding about Lily. Everyone knew that for the next six weeks all they were getting was Paul: an ordinary-looking middle-aged man with grey hair, silver rimmed glasses and surprisingly little self-confidence. Just before leaving Britain, a reporter from the *Guardian* had made the point about how big a gamble Paul was taking by fronting a show under his own name. 'You're not even listed as yourself in our cuttings library,' Paul had been told. 'But Lily's got her own box file.' Redressing the balance would depend entirely on how well this unique travel show was received.

'Go out, and give 'em hell.'

Brendan whispered these key six words at Paul just before the cameras started rolling on the first day of filming. It was what he had told Paul before his first performances as Lily in those raucous south London pubs. It was what he had told him before every television show he had ever appeared in. But it had never seemed as important as it did today. Brendan had been the driving force behind Paul's move out of Lily's shadow. More than almost anyone else in the world he knew the real Paul. He knew that his former lover and lifelong friend didn't actually need a wild persona and a foot-tall beehive on his head to be funny. He knew that Paul had what it took to be a mainstream entertainer in his own right. And as co-producer of *Paul O'Grady's Orient* with Carlton Television, Brendan knew he had to get this message across to its star. It was early in the morning in Singapore but everyone knew the heat was on.

'Ladies and gentlemen, welcome to *Paul O'Grady's Orient*.' Paul had been repeating the phrase endlessly to himself as he tried to build up some rough scripts for the show. He muttered it several times as the crew fussed around the first set of shots outside Raffles but somehow it just didn't feel right. 'I was in smarmy television presenter mode because for some reason I thought I ought to be,' he said. 'I didn't seem to have any persona to fall back on and I didn't have any other example to follow. I was lost for most of that first day.'

Privately the crew admitted that they too could sense that things had fallen surprisingly flat. They needed an edge – and Paul suddenly realised it was looking right back at him in the mirror. He didn't need a persona because he didn't need to try and copy someone from *Wish You Were Here*. 'I just thought, sod it. I'll be Lily Savage without the wig. I didn't want to stand there and talk about economical hotels for families of four because I couldn't care less about families of four. I wanted to talk about what I felt, what I saw, what I knew.' And fortunately for the producers, once Paul started to talk he couldn't stop. The show had momentum – and the next six weeks would be a wonderful rollercoaster.

The producers had lined up a real mix of locations for the series. As well as revisiting many of Paul's old haunts, the idea was to emphasise his unique take on the world and to bring out his natural empathy for the underdog and the oppressed. As well as the plain old weird. 'This is travel, warts and all. Don't expect anything classy. Don't expect no Michael Palin, no Judith Chalmers, no Anthea Turner, none of that business, because you're not getting it,' he crowed at the camera jubilantly as he found his form. And it was certainly hard to imagine Judith in particular mixing with some of Paul's co-stars.

First there were the prostitutes working at his old brothel. Then, in a fantastic episode, came the restaurant owner who served animal penises. Paul checked out how the precious bits of sea lion and sheep were cut up and cooked and decided he didn't feel hungry. The owner, meanwhile, said wistfully that he wanted to try a human penis as well. 'Believe you me, it's not all it's cracked up to be,' Paul replied, with a quick smile to the camera.

Also included in Paul's Orient were pimps, queens and villains. He interviewed Imelda Marcos, sang an impromptu duet with her and off camera said she 'smelled like a funeral parlour'. Then there was the afternoon he went to get his hair cut in Shanghai and ended up being offered sexual favours. 'I thought I was being offered a blow dry, but it turned out to be something else,' he said with a typically arch raising of the eyebrows as the crew fell about laughing behind the cameras.

Paul's willingness to try anything once also got the team through some potentially disastrous moments. In Manila, for example, he ended up dislocating his knee in a nightclub (though to his embarrassment he did it getting off a bar stool, not on the dance floor). After ending up in a wheelchair, Paul agreed to see if a local witch doctor could help – and in the process he turned his accident into pure travel magic. 'She lit some black candles, chanted a bit of jiggery pokery and put her hand on my knee,' he says, admitting that at the time he could hardly hide his scepticism. But something clicked – and it wasn't just his knee. 'The pain just disappeared and I got out of my chair and threw the stick away,' he says. The crew still talk of other crises – including when the whole team were threatened with arrest in Bali for not having all the right work permits.

For all the jokes, the fun and the sheer ridiculousness of some of the scenes – Paul's inability to find the bathroom in his vast Hong Kong hotel suite being a classic example – there were plenty of serious moments as well. One such incident, which Paul knows he could never have tackled as Lily, came when he reached the River Kwai, where 16,000 British prisoners of war had died building the infamous bridge. As a boy Paul had heard the seamen in his family talking long and hard about the forces and the sacrifices so many men had made in the war, and so he knew far more about military history than many might have thought. Three years earlier, when a group of former servicemen protested at the Japanese emperor's 1998 visit to London, an anonymous, soberly dressed Paul O'Grady had joined them in the streets. The old men had so much guts and dignity, he told friends afterwards. And when the old soldiers symbolically turned their backs on the Emperor, so too did Paul. In 2000 in Japan he wanted to raise the issue as he stood beside the bridge.

'But you can't talk about that,' the production team told him, determined to keep the show light.

Paul was horrified. 'How can you ignore something as disgusting as that?' he asked. He launched into a tirade about the so-called compensation paid to British servicemen by the Japanese government – and was furious when most of his words were edited out of the final show. The next moving moment came back in Manila, where Paul started to cry when revisiting the apartment where he had lived as a teenager. 'I used to write letters home to my mum and my friends from there but most of those people aren't around any more. They all died and so I felt like a ghost from another era, like I was intruding on another time.' Sometimes, Paul said afterwards, you find out you really can't go back.

The final point which made *Paul O'Grady's Orient* a milestone for him was that it brought Brendan's first big on-screen appearance – though as introductions go, it was hardly smooth. The pair were caught on camera having a huge row in a massage parlour, of all places. And there viewers learned that both men can talk and argue for Britain.

On the phone to a friend back in London towards the end of the shoot he could hardly contain himself. When asked how it was going he replied, 'It's lovely! I just get up in the morning, have a wash and I'm ready to go.

There's no two hours getting dressed or lugging loads of stuff around for Lily.' Equally importantly, he said, there was none of the pandemonium that comes with filming the six-foot plus blonde bombsite. 'Traffic stops and little kids come up and point when I film in the street as Lily,' he said. 'And can you imagine filming in the Far East in all that heat with a wig, corset and three pairs of tights? It was hot enough without it, thank you very much.'

Then, of course, came Paul's final worry. 'If chewing gum is illegal then wearing heels and two-inch leopardskin miniskirts is probably punishable by death,' he said of Singapore, where the series both began and ended. As the crew prepared for a mini wrap party at the hotel, everyone was convinced that they had done some good work. For all the worries and the doubts, being Paul O'Grady seemed to have paid off. 'Viewers might think that travel shows are one big jolly for everyone but for this one in particular it was a tough filming schedule and everyone worked incredibly hard to make the series a success,' says production manager Sarah Willows. 'But we all knew that no one had more to prove than Paul himself. It was obviously his breakthrough, just as his first appearance on television as Lily had been a decade earlier – you really could tell it meant a great deal to him. There was a huge amount of goodwill on the show, but we all knew we would fall flat on our faces if the viewers didn't get it. And the problem with television is that the long gap between filming and broadcasting means it can take months to find out if you've got a hit or a flop on your hands.'

Feeling both euphoric and exhausted, Paul slumped back down in his business class seat as he flew back to London. He looked over at Brendan and smiled. The pair were both desperately hoping that the new show would be a hit. But even if it wasn't, they knew they had learned a vital lesson. They knew that Paul had found a new voice. He had found the confidence to be himself on screen. A whole new set of possibilities could now open up for them. As the inflight movies began they felt like teenagers again.

Back in Britain, though, the hard graft began almost immediately. The travel show had to be edited and a script written for Paul's voiceovers. As he and Brendan sat in the studio's editing suites working on the post production, Paul was starting to realise just how big a deal it was to be on screen without Lily's war paint. It was clear that his life was probably going to change dramatically when the programme was broadcast. Plain old Paul O'Grady would become a face people recognised when he was out, not just a voice that sometimes sounded vaguely familiar. So could he cope? How easy would it be to face the critics on his own, without Lily's props and her persona to protect him?

James Rampton, a reporter on *The Scotsman* newspaper, was one of the first journalists to catch up with Paul after he came back to Britain and waited to see how the new show would be received. He says it was clear that his interviewee was nervous – but his best guess was that he could cope. 'Paul, like Lily, has balls,' was his simple conclusion after their meeting. In July, after the first episode was broadcast, Paul discovered what it was like to be kicked in them.

When the next day's papers arrived he found the critics were as savage as Paul's former namesake. Paul had 'lost the magic' without Lily, wrote the *Sunday Mirror*'s Ian Hyland. 'Paul O'Grady thinks he is a wit and he is only half right,' offered the *Daily Mail*'s Peter Paterson in his first comments on the show. And these were the best of the bunch. Other commentators took an even tougher line, focusing not just on Paul's personality but the whole structure and style of the show.

'Paul O'Grady should get back into his big girl's blouse. He may be unfunny trash when he is mincing about as Lily Savage, but O'Grady is even worse when he is wearing the trousers,' wrote commentator Tony Parsons in the *Daily Mirror*. '*Paul O'Grady's Orient* was such an embarrassing bit of racism served as light entertainment that it could have been made in the seventies.'

Later in the review, Parsons called Paul 'a narrow-minded moron' before closing with this: 'I wonder what the Chinese made of this strangely effeminate man? "Ah-so," is probably what they murmured. He certainly is, grasshopper.'

By the end of the six-part series things had hardly improved. Peter Paterson was back with even more criticism. '*Paul O'Grady's Orient* must, by a long chalk, be the worst travel series ever shown on British television,' he declared. 'This is a traveller who displays scarcely any interest in the sights he sees, or any pleasure in the human encounters arranged for him. For the first time I can see some merit in the Government's eagerness to remove the passports of our undesirables to prevent them from going abroad and shaming this country,' Paterson concluded, along with news of new plans to discourage travelling football hooligans.

The attacks were particularly hurtful for Paul because he is always fascinated by other people and revels in experiencing new situations. The idea of condemning him as a closet racist was equally extraordinary. What also hurt was the fact that he had never set out to produce a standard travel show, so it seemed wrong to lay into him for not following the rules set by the likes of *Wish You Were Here?* The good news was that the critics seemed out of step with the public. More than six million people watched the first show in the series that July, making it the most popular programme in its timeslot. By the time the final episode was shown, Carlton had signed Paul up for a second series the following year, this time looking at America. The columnists could write whatever they wanted. Paul was getting the last laugh.

Funnily enough his bid to escape Lily wasn't to be quite so funny that autumn. He and a group of friends were doing a bar-crawl around Manchester's Canal Street to celebrate the fact that a second series of the travel show had been commissioned. They were enjoying some drinks in one bar when they got wind of a commotion by the door. A so-called 'celebrity guest' was arriving – it was a lorry driver dressed up as Lily Savage. Hardly able to believe it, Paul and his pals watched as the man waved at all and sundry and started kissing those who rushed up to talk to him. For a while Paul tried to ignore him and focus on his own friends. But when he turned around and saw the new arrival signing autographs for his fellow drinkers, Paul snapped.

'I am not having this,' he said, marching across the bar to where 'Lily' was holding court.

'Can I have an autograph as well?' he asked, his voice taut with anger.

'Who would you like me to make it out to, darling?' the lorry driver asked.

'How about you write: To Paul O'Grady, lots of love, Lily Savage.'

When the man realised what was going on – and, crucially, failed to apologise – Paul lost it again. 'I chinned him and gave him a Liverpool kiss, basically a smack in the gob. My friends had to pull me off him,' he said the next day. The child boxer from Birkenhead had forgotten nothing in the intervening years – and those that crossed Paul would soon see the dangers of underestimating him. 'What got me most annoyed was that he was so hideous, a cross between Myra Hindley and Bet Lynch – and grossly overweight too. He had made no effort, just plonked a wig on his head and put on a cheap frock. It takes me hours to look as gorgeous as I do as Lily and there he was poncing drinks as me.'

The growing band of 'official' Lily Savage lookalikes got better treatment. Having struggled to make a living for so long himself, Paul would never try to make life harder for anyone else who was fighting to get ahead as an entertainer. As long as they were professional about it, then they could earn his blessing.

Helen Neeley, who could make £300 a night on the lookalike circuit as far back as 1999, says the man himself was always supportive of her act – not least because she shared so much with him. She was just a year older than Paul and had also been brought up in a tough Liverpool family. A neighbour had once said she sounded like Lily – and when she put her hair up she realised she could look like her as well. She started off doing a few appearances in pubs and clubs and says she gained a huge respect for both Lily and her creator. When Paul was once bizarrely under fire for being misogynistic Helen was quick to defend him. 'No, Lily does not do a disservice to women. I think she shows a little bit of something that is in all of us but which most of us never have the honesty to show. It's amazing how Paul gets into a woman's thoughts,' she said. And while Helen admits to a momentary worry in the autumn of 2000 that the success of *Paul O'Grady's Orient* might see her character pensioned off, she says there seemed to be no fall-off in demand on the club scene.

For his part, Paul was finding life as himself and as

Lily as busy as ever. He and Brendan realised they needed help running their diaries and keeping their joint shows on the road. Fortunately, one night while chatting in a Soho bar, they reckoned they had found just the man for the job. One of the staff there was a Canadian former police officer called Chad Rogers and while the group were talking they agreed that Chad might be ideally suited to help run Paul's life. After a lot more discussions he was offered the role of Paul's first-ever Personal Assistant – and Chad admits that his life turned upside down.

There were great parties, constant travel, trips to some wonderful hotels and plenty of mixing with celebrities. But there was also a huge amount of hard work. There was a near endless stream of admin and organisation to be done to ensure Paul was never spread too thinly. Paul's key rule is that once he had agreed to a job he will follow through with it. So Chad had to keep a constant eye on his schedule to ensure his boss could always be where he needed to be. He also had to factor in one wild card effect – that while Paul was always determined to be on time for meetings and performances, he also tried to stop and speak to any fans who approached him for autographs or chats. Pulling Paul away from his fans was never easy, not least because Paul usually enjoyed sharing a joke with them and finding out what sort of things were making them laugh or getting them talking. Keeping in touch with the fans keeps his live act fresh, he says.

Chad says interaction with fans was another fun part of his work – and he was constantly amazed at how broad Paul's fan base was, taking in young and old across the country and beyond. Chad would work for Paul for nearly four years before leaving to become PA to a television company executive. But the pair remain firm friends to this day.

'Out of the garage with you.' After a summer in hiding, Lily was back in the autumn for *Lily Live!* on ITV – another hugely stressful series of hour-long shows with a topical edge. The humour was as strong as ever and the newshound in Paul loved scouring the papers for topics that he knew would allow Lily to sound off with abandon. And it worked. The show was nominated for two British Comedy Awards in 2000 – Best Comedy Entertainment Personality and Best Comedy Entertainment Programme.

But this success didn't mean Paul himself was out of the picture. When *Lily Live!* finished he started pre-production of the 2001 follow-up to *Paul O'Grady's Orient*. This time he was to go west to America. And he was going to do it in his own special style. 'Everyone has done the States, which makes it a challenge to find something new. So in each episode we're going to have a stripper!' Paul laughed, just before boarding his plane for the two-month shoot. He would be as good as his word – though he would throw in everyone from cowboys to showgirls as well as he jetted off between

New York, Miami, New Orleans, Dallas, San Francisco and Los Angeles.

The New York adventure was particularly fun. Initially ignoring the bright lights of Broadway for the struggling old burlesque shows in the suburbs, he struck up an instant rapport with the feisty dancers – not all of whom seemed to be in the first flush of youth. Paul was then hoofing it up himself in a high-kicking masterclass from Broadway legend Chita Rivera. Throw in lunch in a flash New York restaurant with old pal Cilla Black and a giggle backstage with Julian Clary who was in the city doing cabaret, and it's easy to see why Paul was happy to smile for the cameras. 'I'm as happy as Carol Vorderman on payday,' he said, taking a sly dig at the star's recent well-publicised contract negotiations with ITV.

But in a moment of television magic the virtual appearance of another British star took the smile off Paul's face. The star in question was Anne Robinson, and Paul stood below a huge poster of her scowling down across Times Square to promote the American version of *The Weakest Link*. 'She thinks she's evil. How can she be evil? She comes from Southport!' he declared, the fellow Scouser in him coming to the fore. And then it was cue the money reference. 'I want that fifteen million quid,' he said of her latest pay deal. 'Why her, when all I've been offered is Snow White in Salford?'

That said, Paul was hardly doing badly himself that spring. Before leaving for America he had trademarked his stage name and entered the rich lists for the first time.

The wealthy experts put his assets at around £4 million, with his half share in the Wildflower production company worth an equal amount. In 2001, just like other comedians from Rowan Atkinson to Jennifer Saunders, Paul was laughing all the way to the bank.

He was also keeping very good company. As the crew joined him in Los Angeles, he met up with Jane Russell, one of his favourite stars from the golden age of Hollywood, and went shopping at glitzy jewellers Harry Winston with Jackie Collins. 'Lily would have filled her pockets but I didn't buy anything,' Paul said afterwards. His own watch cost about ten pence and had been picked up in a market in Bangkok. 'What would I want with something covered in jewels? All I want is to know the time,' he said to the crew, after trying on several near million-dollar timepieces under Jackie's watchful eye.

After the glamour and glitz of LA, it was perhaps little wonder that Paul took advantage of some downtime elsewhere on his trip. And nowhere did he hit the floor quite like in New Orleans. 'It seduced me. It really is the devil's city,' he claimed afterwards.

One example happened on a rare day off when Paul decided to head out of the crew hotel to do some shopping. It was just after midday when he walked past a bar and heard the first bars of *Stormy Weather* being played by a live band. Maybe the shops can wait a little while, he thought, popping in to listen to what was one of his all-time favourite songs. Maybe it's rude to listen without ordering a drink, he thought, as the music played. Maybe I should have another, just so I don't look like some stuffy old Brit. And so it went on.

Four hours later, series director Steve Lennhoff found Paul up on stage in the bar, roaring drunk and singing his heart out. 'Steve said he could hear me five blocks away,' Paul admitted with a very rare blush. In more sober moments in New Orleans Paul went to a jazz festival, on an alligator hunt and to a voodoo ceremony. He met another band of wonderfully wacky people and captured everything on film.

The final surprise of the intense filming schedule was that Paul was disappointed by the one place he had expected to love: San Francisco. 'It was the only place we visited that I didn't like. It's a boring hole – too twee. America is supposed to be the land of the free but San Francisco obviously slipped through the net because there are so many rules. I went to move a stool in one bar and they actually said to me: You can't move that. There's a by-law.'

Glad to leave California, Paul knew bigger challenges faced him at home. He needed to see if this series would be better received than his last one. And unfortunately the knives seemed to be out from the start. The show was: 'clearly just another exercise in transatlantic blagging by presenter and producers in search of a freebie holiday,' said one critic, before any of the series had been broadcast. The early reviews of the first episode were lukewarm at best and by the midway point of the series the die seemed cast.

'O'Grady's tour of American tourist haunts is proving a complete disaster. Thin of content and boorish in presentation,' wrote his old bête noire, Peter Paterson, in the *Daily Mail*. What puzzled Paul most about the overall tone of these reviews was that the writers seemed to have somehow missed his long-standing love of travel. The boy who had sat on his uncles' knees and lapped up stories about exotic destinations had turned into a man thrilled that he had the opportunity to explore so many of those places for real. And the critics who said he patronised some of the places he saw and the people he met seemed equally hard to understand. Paul was the first to admit he loved the high life. But he had never lost his love of life further down the scale. Those at the lowest rung of life's ladder had fascinated him from childhood. They still did. Hanging out with old friends was one other way Paul kept in touch with his past. And later that year he would prove to some of his newer pals that he certainly hadn't forgotten his tough roots.

The evidence came when he headed to the ultra posh Dorchester Hotel on London's Park Lane. Paul had been at the TV Quick Awards and was sitting chatting with former *Coronation Street* actress Tracy Shaw and some other pals at the after-show party. Suddenly, a drunken fellow guest lurched towards them. He clearly fancied Tracy and the group watched embarrassed as his chat-up routine began. Tracy, well used to male attention, was able to humour the guy for a while, but Paul kept an eye on him all the same. So he was watching when the visitor's drunken giggles started to get a little more serious. His jokes were no longer funny and after drinking from some of the spare glasses on Paul and Tracy's table he started to edge ever closer to them.

'Tracy is such a nice, polite girl and she was just putting up with it,' Paul says. 'But then he practically had his hand up her skirt. He was behaving outrageously and I realised I had to protect her.'

'How about you just leave us alone?' Paul's first request was quiet, but there was steel in it.

'Time's up. Time to go,' his next request was clearer. But still the man wouldn't leave, so Paul did what came naturally. He hit him.

'Hang around any longer and I'll give you a lip to match,' Paul said, looking at the man's bruised eye – before having the satisfaction of seeing him practically run from the party. 'If he thought I was just a poof he got the shock of his life,' Paul told a hugely grateful Tracy as they all tried to get on with the rest of their evening.

Actions like this should have given Paul a real boost as summer turned to autumn that year. They proved he was still strong, that he knew right from wrong, that he wasn't afraid of anything and that he would always defend his friends. His dad, he knew, would have been proud of him. But for all this there was something nagging away at the back of his mind. His career was racing ahead again, both as Paul and Lily, and as he started filming the latest set of *Lily Live!* shows he should have been on cloud nine. But in reality, other clouds were starting to swirl around him. They were the black clouds of depression.

The first signs of the black clouds came when Paul found his energy levels could drop sharply and dramatically at any point in the day. The man who says he dreams of the old science fiction idea that you take a pill instead of eating a proper meal found his appetite fell away entirely. So too did his enthusiasm for life and his traditional humour. Everything felt like an effort and nothing he achieved really felt worthwhile. Even his wonderful views in Kent failed to lift his spirits. Looking after his animals didn't seem to be enough to make him feel good.

The first people outside Paul's closely guarded group of friends to see what was going on were Paul's loyal drivers. They were used to the wisecracking, relaxed and caustic wit of the man they said was their favourite passenger. But in the summer of 2001 Paul simply crumpled on the back seat and waved the car on. One day on the journey from Kent to the television studio he simply dissolved in a fit of tears – and this then became a regular feature of his near-daily journeys. Once Paul arrived at the south bank studio complex it was equally hard to pretend that all was well. His eyes were puffy and bloodshot and his mood was black – something his inner circle tried desperately to keep under wraps. Paul remembers one terrible day when the staff had to practically push him into a cupboard to hide so that none of the others would see how close he was to falling apart.

But, amazingly, Paul never once failed to deliver star quality when the moment came to perform – though he still can't quite explain how this happened. 'It was extraordinary. I would get on stage and Lily would be crackling, at her most vitriolic, mouthy and strong,' he remembers. The audiences loved it and the production team applauded as their star headed back to the dressing room. But when the lights clicked off and the cameras stopped rolling, Paul's personal shutters came down fast. He would get changed in silence and walk fast, head down, to his car so that he could be taken home as quickly as possible.

'Paul, mate, what's the problem? Is it drugs? Is it booze? Is it sex-related?'

Looking back, Paul lost count of the times his closest friends and colleagues begged for clues. Everyone wanted to help him – they wanted to bring back the Paul O'Grady they loved, the one who was always ready with a joke or an anecdote and who would make fun of himself if no other targets were available. Some of those who spotted the classic signs of depression advised their friend to consider Prozac or therapy as a way out of his black hole. But Paul refused: 'You can't run away from your problems.'

And to his credit Paul tried desperately hard not to wallow in self-pity, even though he had no idea what was going on inside his head. 'I was at my lowest ebb.

I tried to rationalise it. God, here I was with this great career, a beautiful home surrounded by animals, everything I ever wanted. I've got a swimming pool, cars to drive me to work and people running around after me. But I'd wake up miserable, inert, and I'd drag myself up and go through the motions.'

What made matters worse was that a quirk in the television schedules seemed to devalue Paul's work and bring him some unfairly negative reviews. Several of the *Lily Live!* shows he was working on when the depression first hit him were held back for several weeks before being broadcast. And the delays didn't do them any favours. 'Not only was Lily not live, she was not funny either,' wrote one TV critic, unwittingly landing a punch on the show's star when he was already a long way down.

One of his friends, Sue Carroll from the *Daily Mirror*, remembers how hard Paul struggled with his demons, not least because his natural inclination was to dismiss any form of mental issues as self-indulgent. 'The clouds just descended on me from nowhere,' Sue remembers him telling her almost in a whisper. 'It was bleakness from the moment I woke up until I went to bed. Before it happened, if anyone came to me and said they were depressed I would just say, "Pull yourself together." That's the kind of background I'm from. No one in my family ever got maudlin or depressed. It just wasn't done.'

What the O'Grady clan and their feisty neighbours

did do was to try and dismiss any problems with a clever word or a well-placed punchline. So Paul thought back to his parents, to his aunties Chrissy and Annie in Birkenhead, and the brilliant one-liners they conjured up when everything around them looked bleak. Humour was his family backbone. He would try and use it to pull himself back on to his feet. So when one of his friends again suggested he see a friendly therapist Paul finally felt ready to say no with a smile. 'What can some bearded hippie years younger than me with dubious qualifications know about me or my lifestyle? After the life I've led there's no one qualified enough to take me on – it would have to be Jung or Freud themselves,' he said, feeling just a tiny bit better as the repartee began to flow again.

More important to his slow recovery was the time he spent on his farm. That late summer day in 1999, when he had first collected the keys, he had predicted that it would be his refuge from the world. He was right, and two years later it began teaching him vital lessons. On his blackest days he would think back to how some of his animals had behaved when they had been ill or injured. They had stopped eating. They had stopped moving. His dogs, in particular, would just crawl under a table and wait for recovery to come. 'I can do that. I'll ride this one out,' Paul thought, as he fussed around them. He would have faith, just as they did, that recovery would ultimately come. What Paul wouldn't do, he swore, was to turn to booze to prop him up and keep him going.

Some sense of self-preservation deep inside him told him that this would only make life harder.

'Every morning I would give myself a bollocking. I'd say, "What right have you got to feel down? You're not living in a squat with a houseful of hungry kids. You used to be a social worker. You've seen it all. You used to wipe arses at 6am and whistle while you did it. Now all you have to do is slap around in stilettos and earn silly money. Get a grip." I was tough on myself, mentally and physically. Somehow I knew I had to be.'

Funnily enough, the on-off double life that Paul had led since childhood was to help him get through this low patch. The man who was Paul one moment and Lily the next had to undertake similar transformations on the road to recovery. So in the mornings, he says, he would be his own worst enemy, berating himself for self-pity and pushing himself on through his day. In the evenings he would switch to being his own best friend, praising himself for any small successes and making it through the day. Apart from all the tough love, he knew he had to take time to give himself the occasional pat on the back.

But how long would this desperate depression last? Paul admits there were days when he felt the clouds might never lift – there were certainly days back then when he could barely remember a time when they hadn't been swirling all around him. They were like the Death Eaters in Harry Potter, he said, sucking the life and the colour out of everything around them. And Paul had no magic wand or trickery to send them back to Azkaban.

Fortunately, though, one crisp autumn morning Paul woke up and felt alive again. He got out of bed feeling unaccountably hungry, looking forward to speaking to his friends and glad he had something in his diary for the afternoon. He hadn't felt like this for several months – and he had forgotten how good it was. As that first day of recovery progressed he tried to take things slowly, just in case the good mood didn't last. But the following day he woke up and found his head was still clear and the hunger was still there. By the weekend he was really starting to feel alive again. No longer did he want to lock himself away in his farmhouse and keep the curtains shut tight. He wanted to be in the fresh air and surrounded by noisy, lively people again. Best of all, his irrational fears about the future seemed to have disappeared and he was ready to enjoy the moment. It seemed as if depression had left him, just as quickly as it had arrived. He was euphoric.

Once more, Paul's drivers were among the first to spot the recovery. Their favourite passenger was once more cracking jokes, leering at pedestrians, fellow motorists and – his favourite targets – cyclists as they swept up to London and back. He was talking loudly on his phone and commenting on almost everything he read in the papers and magazines on the back seat. Paul O'Grady was back in business, and he was determined to stay that way.

What he needed to do, he realised, was to try and remember exactly how he had felt when the low times had first hit. He wanted to pinpoint any triggers, to analyse how it had affected him and how he had dug himself out of the deepest troughs. He wanted to be aware of the warning signs so that he could take early action if they ever returned. Next time, he feared, it could take a lot longer to shift and so he wanted to be ready.

What he still refused to do, he told friends, was to see a psychiatrist. 'If I'd had counselling when I was depressed I'd have lied, I know I would. I'd have told them I wanted to steal a baby. I'd have made something up to justify their existence.' Instead, solid self-reliance and good, patient friends would see Paul through his crises. That and the one thing that had always saved him in the past: hard work.

'Are we really ready for this? I need another toilet break!' Paul was in a tiny dressing room backstage at the Dominion Theatre in London as he got back into the swing of things with a bang. It was just before 11am on the morning of the Royal Variety Performance and Paul was excited and terrified in equal measure. So were the two old friends squeezed into the dressing room with him – Cilla Black and Barbara Windsor. The trio had sneaked into the theatre an hour earlier trying to hide their faces from the hardy group of fans who were already gathered around the stage door. None had stopped to sign autographs or pose for pictures – because their inclusion in the show was supposed to be top secret.

In 2001, Elton John, Jennifer Lopez, Cher and the men

from *The Full Monty* were the big headline acts. But Paul, Cilla and Barbara would win the biggest headlines the next day. The trio had decided to do a very special rendition of *You Gotta Have A Gimmick*, a show-stopping number from *Gypsy*, one of Paul's all-time favourite musicals. And what a gimmick they had. Paul was in Lily mode, and all three of them would be wearing some seriously sexy costumes. Black basques, suspenders and sheer silk stockings – and hidden lights all over their bodies, which would flick on and flash at a crucial moment in the act.

If it all went according to plan, it would be a triumph – proof that even at a certain age all three performers were still at the top of their games. But would things go to plan? Barbara for one is happy to admit that the pals had struggled to find enough time for rehearsals. And that even on the day of the show they kept getting distracted. 'We kept running off and going to the loo together,' she jokes about the final hours before the Queen and the Duke of Edinburgh took their seats in the Royal Box. More seriously, everyone knew that however naff their public image might have become, Royal Variety Performances were no places for mistakes.

'If you are directing or managing a show with celebrity guests or performers then you have to be ready for tantrums, hissy fits, delays and endless disruptions,' says theatre manager Marsha South. 'But when you have the Queen in the audience you play to a higher level. The police presence, both uniformed and plain clothed, plus the diplomatic protection officers and all the other parts of the entourage mean that there is no room for error. You can't have delays. You can't mess up. However cynical you might be about royalty or however little you profess to care about the Queen, you can't ignore the huge extra buzz that is generated when she's in the building. It's a fact of life and it affects everyone.'

Little wonder, then, that there were a few more mad dashes to the loo just before Paul, Cilla and Barbara did their extraordinary burlesque act. Little wonder as well that there were such huge cheers when they took their curtain calls. They had been billed as a surprise special act. They hadn't disappointed. Just over 11.5 million viewers tuned into the performance in 2001, the show's highest television audience in five years. When Paul was on stage the ratings analysts said nearly half of all television viewers were watching the show. So all those people who had been wondering where Paul was during his depression that autumn were finally given their answer. He was back. And with a clear mind and a new lease of life, he was ready to hit the studios with a vengeance.

His first task was to start work on the next twenty episodes of *Blankety Blank*. The team had been set a cracking pace with several shows due to be completed a day towards the end of the run, but after his miserable autumn Paul was up to the challenge. He was thriving again and life felt fantastic. What he didn't know was that it was about to deal him the biggest blow of all.

CHAPTER NINE
Warning Bells

'Lily, I've got a present for you!' Wendy Clamp was in the contestant's chair as the latest *Blankety Blank* recording began. Lily had already had the studio audience and the celebrity guests rocking with laughter after taking the mickey out of Wendy's fiancé – who was an undertaker. And as far as he was concerned this joke could run and run.

'I hope it's not embalming fluid or something,' Lily retorted, with a trademark sneer. It wasn't – but it might as well have been. As the audience's laughter levels hit another peak Wendy handed over a specially made miniature coffin with the name Lily Savage cut neatly into the lid.

'How lovely. I don't know what to say,' Lily replied,

with a typically arch look at the cameras as she made a big scene of pushing the gift away in disgust.

'Okay, pull yourselves together. Heart: Blank.' Ten minutes had passed, and Lily moved across to the panel and approached *Peak Practice* actor Gray O'Brien as the game began. 'Attack?' Gary offered tentatively.

'First the coffin. Now you say "heart attack". It's a cheerful show, isn't it?' Lily said, having the time of her life now that the jokes were starting to flow.

But had all the talk of illness and death struck a chord? Two nights later Paul was at a charity dinner in aid of gay rights group Stonewall at the Dorchester Hotel in London. One of his fellow guests was *EastEnders* actor-turned MEP Michael Cashman – a man Paul now thought of as a close friend. 'Paul was in really good form, very funny as usual and looking fine,' Michael said afterwards. But he admits that the tone of their conversation did turn uncharacteristically dark when they headed down to the hotel bar for a few drinks after the meal.

'We're not teenagers any longer,' Michael said ruefully, as they discussed the pressures of work and how important it was to slow down sometimes.

'Listen kid, we've got to promise to ourselves that we will look after one another,' Paul replied just after midnight as the pair said their goodbyes. The streets were still surprisingly full as Paul's car took him down Park Lane, past Buckingham Palace and the House of Commons and over Tower Bridge to his London home.

He never tired of those iconic sights, though on the 18 April, 2002 he was feeling just a little too tired to really appreciate them. While he could have dozed in the back of the car, he was glad he had decided to stay in town that night, rather than heading down to Kent. I'll sleep like a baby tonight, he thought, as he waved his driver goodbye and headed to his bed. But he was wrong.

Within an hour Paul was wide awake and he knew, instantly, that something was wrong. His mind was racing and while the sweat poured off his body he started to vomit. This wasn't the booze coming out, he knew, not least because he had hardly touched the stuff that night. This was far more serious. Desperate to stay calm he dragged himself to his sofa and his phone, just in case. Lying down there to catch his breath he suddenly felt an excruciating pain surge up his arm. 'It was like someone had put pliers up my arm and squeezed. I've never felt pain like it,' he said afterwards. At the time though he thought something else: 'This is it. I've had it.' Paul had seen his dad suffer a fatal heart attack in a hospital corridor within hours of his mother's attack. He had seen so many other family members suffering with their hearts. He knew that history was repeating itself. He too was having a heart attack and it felt like a big one.

'This is it. I've had it.'

The six words echoed around Paul's mind again as the sweats and the vomiting intensified. But then he made a vow to drown out his fears. He had been a fighter all his life. He would fight this as well. Trying desperately to ignore the pains in his body he found his phone. He called Brendan, his one true emergency service, and Brendan dialled 999.

In the ambulance there was drama, humour, and an extraordinary sense of calmness. The paramedics said Paul was officially dead for ten seconds, and later, when he was able to crack weak jokes about it, he says he was disappointed not to see any angels, tunnels or blinding white lights on his voyage. What he does remember is regaining consciousness to find the ambulance man trying to force a blood-thinning aspirin into his mouth. He also remembers, bashfully, what he did next. He bit him. More seriously, Paul remembers feeling strangely calm with absolutely no fear of death. 'Apparently we have a mechanism in us that calms us down and prepares us for death. I thought I would be thinking, "Why is this happening to me?" But I wasn't. I've never been scared of dying and I wasn't then. I just lay there, thinking: "You've had a good innings, O'Grady, and you've got away with absolute murder, so be grateful."'

He was also surprisingly aware of everything that was going on around him – and he had to say he approved of it. 'I said to myself: "You're going out in a blaze of glory, with an ambulance siren going and a copper on a motorbike escorting you at 3am after coming from the Dorchester."' The boy from Birkenhead had certainly done good, he felt. If this was his time to go, then he was at least taking his curtain call in style. But by the time the ambulance arrived at St Thomas's Hospital beside

Westminster Bridge, Paul's mood had toughened. There would be another act in his life, he vowed. He wasn't ready to go after all. With Brendan at his side as his trolley was rushed down towards the coronary care unit Paul was up for a fight.

The hospital staff worked with skilled precision in the first few moments as Paul was re-assessed. He was injected with diamorphine to dull the pain and given other jabs to deal with the increasing nausea that characterises a heart attack. He was then whisked to the angiography suite where a team of cardiologists injected colourings into his arteries so that they could spot and target the blockages. He had stents (tiny mesh tubes) inserted to keep the blood flowing to his heart – with everything caught on camera and shown on a screen above the bed so that the entire medical team could keep tabs on exactly what was going on.

'Nurse, can I have a ciggie?'

It was only half a joke as Paul tried to take his mind off the operation. He smiled his thanks as the nurse gave him a pencil to suck on instead. There is something totally bizarre about all this, he thought a little later as he lay back on the bed and looked up at the television screen. It's like going to a very posh dinner party and then watching a film afterwards. He just wished his arteries weren't in a starring role.

Brendan had spent much of the first few hours after Paul's admittance on the phone, and shocked family and friends were soon rallying around. Sharyn cancelled her holiday, rushed down to London and after seeing her dad in his hospital bed, demanded that he ring her every day to tell her how he was feeling. Cilla Black heard the news while at her holiday home in Barbados and also said she wanted to fly straight back to visit him. Old pal Amanda Mealing was also one of the first in Paul's intensive care ward. She brought his baby godson, Milo and started to cry almost the moment she arrived – something that in itself served as a wake-up call for Paul. 'I'd never seen her cry before,' he realised, soberly. 'It made me realise how serious it was.'

Other famous names who were on hand to offer their support included the legendary Lauren Bacall and Kim Cattrall – both rang Paul direct as soon as they heard about his attack. Another early visitor was the famously hard-living Rolling Stone Ronnie Wood. 'Game's up, lads. We've got to behave ourselves from now on,' the pair agreed, as they talked softly about their lives and their health.

But as a testament to just how well-loved Paul had become, he says one of the visitors who meant the most to him was someone very far from the public eye. It was the man who sweeps the roads near Tower Bridge who Paul chatted to whenever he was out walking Buster. 'He just wanted to know I was doing okay and to say he hoped I was back out with the dog soon,' Paul said afterwards, almost brought to tears by the gesture. 'The whole outpouring of emotion from so many wonderful people really made me cry and in some ways it was worse than the heart attack itself. For some reason I find it hard when people are being nice to me.' As a man who was now so clearly loved he would have to get used to it.

Ultimately, Paul said he put the heart attack down to the 'four c's' – cigarettes, cholesterol, caffeine and Carlton Television. The doctors added a fourth – congenital – and they said it carried a very serious message. 'They said I was a timebomb waiting to go off,' Paul admitted. 'At forty-six they said I had the heart of an old man. And of course I can hardly forget that heart disease was what killed both my mum and my dad.' He was also keenly aware that his elder brother had already suffered his own episodes of heart trouble, that one of his cousins had a pacemaker and that his sister had angina. 'When the hearts were handed out to our family they gave us the job lot of pokey old ones,' he said, trying to make light of the situation.

As he waited for the latest test results on his own heart he was warned to prepare himself for a triple by-pass operation – one of the most gruelling and risky pieces of cardiac surgery, which in the end was considered unnecessary. He also had to face the strange sensation – it felt like an out of body experience – of watching news reports of his own hospitalisation on the television in his room. It was like hearing your own obituary being read in front of you, he told his visitors quietly. 'I've used up another of my nine lives,' he admitted to them, as he tried to stop them fussing or worrying too much. But he refused to say exactly how many he felt he had left.

More serious were his thoughts about the medical staff he had dealt with since that first early-morning 999 call. The NHS had been utterly wonderful, he said, and once he was in hospital the nurses in particular had reaffirmed his faith in humanity. They also brought some new perspective to his life. 'To say that they deserve a medal is an understatement. I looked at the work they were doing and felt ashamed. I thought of the meaningless work I do and what I get paid for it and thought, "This is disgusting." The world of telly makes you hard and cynical and something like this really gets to you. I won't forget,' he vowed.

As anyone who has suffered a heart attack will attest, being discharged from hospital does not necessarily mean the worst is over. Like anyone else, Paul headed home with a tough new medication regime to face and its effects brought as many bad days as good. They also brought some shocks – when he accidentally cut his finger one day opening his living room window, he couldn't believe how much his blood-thinning tablets made him bleed. As the drugs kicked in, Paul also found himself crying for what felt like no reason at any time of the day or night. He shed tears he said he hardly knew he had in him. But he knew he still had much to be thankful for. What brought this home more than almost anything else were the sackloads of letters and cards he was still receiving from fans. The first cards had been hand-delivered to the hospital within 24 hours of his admittance. Since then whole classes of schoolkids had signed notes and letters, little old ladies had sent good wishes addressed simply to Lily Savage, London, and people of all ages and backgrounds seemed to be passing on their best wishes and health tips for the future.

As he tried to rebuild his strength, Paul was forced to do something he had spent his whole career trying to avoid: he had to go back on a promise. He was being named top TV personality at the Heritage Foundation Awards at London's Grosvenor House Hotel and was due to be in the audience along with Bruce Forsyth, Amanda Barrie and Wendy Richard, but his doctors said a big night out would be too dangerous – and Paul knew they were right. The man who prided himself on turning up on time and performing even through his tears was distraught at the thought of letting the Foundation staff down. But he knew that for once he had to listen to his doctors, rather than to the sergeant major in his mind. Cancelling the gig turned out to be the right thing to do because more than a fortnight later, when he finally felt ready for a private night out, he received a stark reminder of how fragile he was. He went to see a play at a theatre in Marlow but came home so exhausted it took him nearly another full week to regain his strength.

'What you need is a holiday.' Brendan made the decision later that summer and while things didn't exactly go to plan, the trip did seem to help Paul rediscover his sense of humour. The pair headed out to the Italian Riviera and Paul started complaining from the moment they arrived. 'I hated it! We were only a day in each place and I had two suitcases that I had to lug everywhere. I had no energy and the sweat was just running off me – it was like being on bloody *Tenko*. All we did was row, so it wasn't a good idea.'

What was a good idea was to relax at home instead. With so much beautiful countryside around his Kent farm and his beloved Saxon Shore Way to walk, Paul knew that he couldn't find a better place to regain his strength.

The only cloud on the horizon that year was the news that Paul wasn't the only one wandering around the beautiful Kent fields. Police were called amid rumours that an obsessed fan was in the area trying to get on to Paul's land. 'You haven't made it until you've got a stalker,' he told the *Sunday Mirror*, trying to make light of the story. The gentle humour seemed to work and after the authorities started to make regular checks on Paul's property, the fan gave up his vigil and disappeared. Part of the relief Paul felt when the police told him that the threat had passed came from the fact that he hated having to cut himself off from fans or to put any distance between himself and the public. He had been brought up with an old-fashioned view of the fame game – thinking it brought both rights and responsibilities to each side.

'I don't see the point in wearing a baseball cap and dark glasses – they're like putting a giant sign up saying: Look at me! Anyway, part of the job we do as entertainers is to be recognised and you have to accept that,' he said. He knew he was extraordinarily well paid for what he did. So the least he could do was acknowledge the people who paid his wages when they decided they wanted to say hello.

That summer, a reinvigorated Paul was busy meeting plenty of new people as he threw himself into a host of new activities. He learned to swim, he thought about learning to fly, and he even considered learning the trumpet. What he absolutely refused to do any more was sit still or wrap himself up in cotton wool. 'My heart attack was my wake-up call. Now all I want to do is try new things, new challenges. I'm still alive and I want to make the most of everything,' he declared.

As usual, he also wanted to make a joke out of everything – and he began with his super-healthy new diet. 'I'm eating so much fish oil I think I might turn into a bleeding mackerel,' he told friends. And the rice milk, low-fat spreads and tofu cheeses were bringing a character change of their own. Paul O'Grady the hippy was just one calorie-free veggie-burger away. 'If I'm not careful I'll soon be making angora goats' hair jumpers and selling pan pipes at the garden gate.' He also joked that his alter ego was now less Lily Savage and more Snow White. 'It's all clean bloody living. No drink or drugs and I'm tucked up in bed by ten. Who'd have thought it?'

Jokes apart, Paul did still have one private struggle to contend with. The lifelong smoker felt he owed it to his doctors and nurses to give up. He told himself that if he ever ended up back in hospital because of a smoking-related illness, he would feel as if he had betrayed them all. So whenever he wanted a cigarette he tried to think of the individual nurses who had put him back together again. Light up and it will be as if you are spitting in all their faces, he told himself. But the man who once joked that the two great loves of his life were 'Benson' and 'Hedges' was still struggling every day with the addiction. In the past he had said that he hadn't been able to answer the phone, let alone write a joke, without a cigarette in his hand. Today the urge was as strong as ever. He saw a hypnotist, took advice from as many ex-smokers as he could find and slapped on so many nicotine patches that he ended up suffering nightmares, weird dreams and daytime confusions. His doctors had already put him on beta-blockers to try and calm him down, but they too started to make him feel depressed. So he threw them all away. His Birkenhead childhood had taught self-reliance above all else. So he vowed to get through this crisis without any artificial help.

Ultimately, Paul would go from full strength cigarettes to Silk Cut. Then he would try to cut these back in stages as well, first stopping himself from smoking in the car, then making his house off-limits as well. At times he wondered if it was worth it – because like many lifelong smokers he found he was constantly overwhelmed by fits of coughing as his lungs got used to the feel of clean air and started to expel a lifetime of tar and mucus. 'I've never had a cough in my life. I give up smoking and I'm coughing my guts up like I'm on 2,000 a day. So much for healthy bloody living,' he joked. The struggle to give up cigarettes would be one he would never truly win. But he knew how important it was to keep trying. 'I swore I would stop and I hate breaking promises. I said I would do it not just for me but for all those people who saved my life,' he said, once more proving how hard he could drive himself to please others.

By the late summer Paul was finally ready to move on. He told reporters he no longer wanted to talk about his health and he didn't want to become some sort of poster boy for heart disease. What he did want to talk about was television – and how awful it was. 'The rubbish I have watched! I didn't realise daytime TV was so bad,' he told *Daily Mirror* writer Alun Palmer. 'It rots your brain quicker than smack. Have you ever seen such utter crap? All these makeover shows – nothing will induce me to turn an orange box into a handy bedside cabinet, not while Ikea is around. It's all too traumatic. I have to get back to work,' Alun remembers him saying.

Fortunately for Paul there were plenty of people with faith in him, and plenty of high-profile opportunities to grasp. His first job was to present a gong at the British Soap Awards, where the celebrity audience gave him a standing ovation when he walked out from the wings – as himself rather than as Lily. But it wasn't his fellow celebrities Paul was thinking about as the clapping finally ended. It was all the viewers and fans who had supported him since that awful April night. 'I've had so many cards, letters, and dolls and teddy bears from people. And I've had flowers, flowers, flowers. I'd like to say from the bottom of my now-mended heart, thank you very much,' he said, as the tears started to flow.

Mended or not, most people in the television world expected that Paul's next move would be to play things safe. A new gameshow, perhaps, or a light talk show that could ease him back into the world of work in familiar surroundings. Paul had other ideas. A theatre producer called Michael Rose had been in touch. He wanted to see if Paul felt up to a twelve-week run in one of the biggest musical hits on the London stage. The show was *Chitty Chitty Bang Bang* at the London Palladium and Michael was convinced that Paul would make a fantastic Child Catcher. 'It was a long shot asking Paul to take on the part bearing in mind what had just happened to him, but we're all incredibly excited about seeing him on stage,' Michael told the press when Paul threw caution to the wind and signed up. Just six months after his April heart attack and he was heading back to the stage.

The costume fittings and make-up sessions were hilarious. Paul's face was pale and malicious in his top-to-toe black cloaks. 'He looks like a praying mantis,' said a delighted Michael Rose. But looking the part was only half the battle. Paul had to live it – eight times a week in front of a little less than 2,000 people a time on one of the most prestigious stages in the world. The big challenge was that the role had to be played entirely straight. There was no humour in it. No light-hearted asides, no ad-libs, no playing to the gallery and lightening of the mood. 'Pure evil,' is how Paul saw it, admitting that he had always been terrified of the original film. And while the Child Catcher only had a relatively minor role, Paul was also pretty scared about appearing alongside the show's original stars Michael Ball and Brian Blessed.

'Looking back, it is hard to underestimate how big a career challenge this was for Paul and he deserved a lot of respect for taking it on,' says theatrical agent Millie Palmer. 'Just because he was on stage in yet another outrageous costume doesn't mean he was in his usual comfort zone. This wasn't about being Lily Savage or Paul O'Grady. It was straight theatrical acting, playing an entirely new role in which he could have been totally unconvincing. And as he was playing alongside a cast that had a huge heritage in musical theatre, any shortcomings on Paul's part would have stuck out like a sore thumb. Being the Child Catcher wasn't just a gruelling job so soon after his heart attack, it was also a huge gamble for him, for the producers and all the other stars in the show.'

Fortunately it was a gamble everyone would win. Paul's arrival in the cast triggered a new set of reviews in all the national newspapers. All of them were good. *Chitty Chitty Bang Bang* had already been playing to full houses. Soon there would be an even longer line for returns outside the theatre.

Allowing himself what was now a rare glass of

champagne in his dressing room after his opening night Paul was feeling on top of the world and ready for anything. Including his journey home. 'The city is a war zone at night nowadays,' he declared, appalled at the anti-social and threatening behaviour he saw all around him. 'I'm going home on the night bus in full costume to scare the living daylights out them,' he laughed.

As the weeks passed Paul found his new role incredibly invigorating. Being forced to stick to his character and his script wasn't a problem and it seemed to free his mind to be more creative about the other roles he wanted to play. And that meant the possible return of the Savage. 'No, I haven't got sick of her and no, she isn't gone for good,' he told reporters. But as usual he felt she was ready to evolve, as all true comedy characters must. And she could do so by incorporating his own health scare into her act.

'My God, she got a shock when I told her she had to give up fags, booze and dirty men,' he joked, playing out new scenes in his mind as he talked. And if he did ever have to go back to hospital for some more remedial surgery, then he knew he could get some laughs out of that as well. 'She'll delight in having a low cut frock, going, "Look at my scars. I only went in for a verruca and the bastard's knife slipped."' But as it turned out Paul's plans for Lily were to go on hold that long, exhausting autumn. Something else was to take precedence. He wasn't the only one to be in hospital fighting for his life.

'I'm pregnant again. And I've got breast cancer.'

It was one of the most awful phone conversations Paul can ever remember. But when his old pal Amanda Mealing gave him her news he was ready to drop everything to support her. He joined forces with Amanda's husband Richard and her other family and friends to see her through the final months of her pregnancy, when doctors were unable to do anything about the cancer. And he was right there to help after baby Otis was born and Amanda was taken back to hospital to have her breast removed and to start chemotherapy.

What amazed and inspired Paul the most was his friend's ability to face up to the situation without a trace of self-pity. And he knew his role was simply to be there for her – just as she had been for him after his heart attack. 'We would just sit and talk rubbish together. We'd rip people to shreds, usually the ones we had been working with most recently. So it was all: "Oh, bloody BBC." We never shut up.'

After her operations and during the worst of her treatment, Paul took Amanda down to his farm in Kent and tried to make the most comforting comfort food he could think of – she says his shepherd's pie was among the best she had ever tasted. 'While I rested he would take my boys out for the day,' Amanda remembers. 'Then as soon as I woke up he was there with a drink. And he was always giving me little incentives. As soon as you're well enough, he'd say, I'm going to take you to Paris or wherever.' Paul and Richard remained thick as thieves during the illness and everyone felt like one huge family – a happy one, despite the awful circumstances that had brought them together under the same Kent roof.

When Amanda, Richard, Milo and baby Otis all headed back to their home in Lincolnshire Paul's protective instincts were far from over. Amanda had posed for some photographs, showing her scars, to try and raise awareness of cancer and to help other women see that the disease needn't be a death sentence. But Paul found that the public reaction wasn't always very positive. 'I'd sat in my dressing room and sobbed when I saw the pictures. But once, I saw some old woman was looking at them and I heard her say: "Isn't that disgusting?" So I went for her, tooth and nail. "Let's hope you never have to have your breasts off, you mealy mouthed old bitch," I told her.' It was a rare, verbal attack on a complete stranger. But it proved once more that Paul can be one of the fiercest of friends anyone could have. And one of the worst of enemies.

On a far lighter note, Paul carried on making himself the butt of his own jokes – including at the recording of the BBC's *Best Moments of 2002* ceremony, where he hung out with pal Sue Johnston. To this day the pair still compete over which of them made the biggest fool of themselves when they went back stage and met their joint heroine Liza Minnelli.

'I am so honoured to meet you. I saw you in Hamburg,' was Paul's bold opening gambit.

'I thought you were wonderful when I saw you at the

Manchester Apollo,' followed up Sue, as Liza silently offered her hand and then moved sharply on.

'How embarrassing are we?' Paul asked Sue afterwards. 'We behaved like school kids meeting our idol. I was practically curtseying to her. She couldn't get rid of us quick enough.'

With his run in *Chitty Chitty Bang Bang* now over, Paul was ready for another challenge. Or at least he thought he was. The challenge he picked was panto and with hindsight it was to prove one gruelling job too many. For the fourth year in a row Paul signed up to play the Wicked Queen in *Snow White* – this time at the Manchester Opera House. But with his opening night coming less than eight months after his heart attack and so soon after his Child Catcher performances, a tiny part of him worried that the two shows a day routine might be too much for him.

'Slow down, calm down, take it easy,' he told himself. 'You don't want to drop dead and be taken to hospital dressed as a wicked queen with seven dwarfs running along behind you. That's not very dignified, Paul,' he said. But the show's workload was relentless and Paul refused to give less than 100 per cent in any performance. At the end of each night he knew he had to catch up on his rest and start taking better care of himself. But he was in a terrible vicious circle. The more tired he got, the harder, somehow, it became for him to sleep. And the man who says he sees food as a necessity, and who only has to miss a single meal if he wants to lose weight, sometimes found himself missing every meal of the day. Often it was because he felt too tired to shop. But on other days it was because he was too tired even to eat. After such a long stint in the theatre dressing and rehearsal rooms in London and Manchester, he started to pick up some of the bugs that were always around.

Too exhausted to exercise properly, he craved the fresh air and winter winds of his Kentish retreat. But there always seemed another noisy matinee to start, another sold-out evening show to prepare for. When he weighed himself one night after a show he found that he was around two stones below his pre-heart attack level of thirteen stone. He also didn't like the look of the pale, washed-out face he saw in the mirror in front of him. But as usual he refused to give in. He had signed a contract to do this panto, so that was that. He would work as hard as ever until the end of the run. He could cope, he told himself. Or at least he could until he opened one of the tabloid newspapers that January.

There was a photograph of him wrapped up against the cold, walking down a Manchester street and looking, frankly, terrible. But far worse were the words that accompanied the picture. They were cleverly written, to fend off any legal problems. But the message was pretty clear. 'The implication was that I was at death's door. It was a case of "Gay man of a certain age loses weight; it must be Aids". It was evil, pure evil. On top of that they made out I was in hiding, like some sort of latter-day Greta Garbo, a sad and lonely recluse. I was livid,' said Paul, literally shaking with anger.

But what upset him even more was that so many people believed it. His phone started to ring almost non-stop from people who wanted to know how he was and how they could help. Even a distraught Sharyn rang up in tears after reading one report – she actually asked her dad if it was true he was dying of cancer. 'Don't you think I would have told you if that was the case? It's all a load of nonsense,' he said, trying to make light of it. 'Bad living keeps me thin, you know that.'

But still the rumour mill turned. Still the nasty insinuations were made. 'I felt like having a blood test to prove everyone wrong but then I thought: Why should I? I'm not answerable to anyone.' And his sister told him he was right. 'Tell them all to go to shite,' was her typically forthright advice.

So that, in the end, was what Paul did. He braved out the storm, worked out his contract in Manchester, led the endless curtain calls at the final performance and then headed back south to relax and recover in his own time. In the process, he dumbfounded his friends by discovering an appetite for food. The man they said had only ever gone to restaurants in order to bitch about the décor or check out the waiters seemed only to have eyes for the menu. He joked he could easily eat his own quickly increasing body weight, racing through as many courses as he could find time for. 'I've actually got a neck,' he joked. And this wasn't all – after a massive new exercise campaign he found out he had muscles. He swam almost every day, went cycling and took karate lessons (while imagining himself as a character from his childhood favourite *The Avengers*). He rode horses round his fields and even set up a gym in his garden shed. It soon started to have an effect.

'Paul, since when did you have tits?'

'What are you talking about?'

'Look in the mirror.'

Paul was at home with a friend when his fitness regime took root. And as he followed his pal's instructions he had to admit he was right. 'I've always been built like a knitting needle but it was true. I did have tits,' he says. 'So the next time you see Lily Savage she will look like one of those Russian athletes. Just a mass of sinew and muscle.'

Once more, a host of new sketch opportunities opened up in Paul's mind as he looked at his reflection. Life really couldn't be better – and he soon got an even bigger boost when his doctor told him he had never been leaner or fitter. 'You heart is finally a credit to you,' Paul was told, after having a full ultrasound and 24-hour ECG test. And his medication could finally reflect it. The ten pills a day he had been taking immediately after his heart attack had already been reduced to just two, to tackle his blood pressure. Then they were no longer deemed necessary either. 'When they put me on a treadmill for my annual check up the doctor said I was four stages above average. Plenty of his other patients became couch potatoes after their heart attacks, apparently. But I was out hiking and it turned out to have been exactly the right thing to do,' says Paul.

Back in London, however, he admits he was also out doing slightly less innocent pursuits. For reasons really known only to himself, in 2003 the American illusionist David Blaine had decided to spend 44 days suspended in a glass box on the edge of the Thames near Paul's house. The crowds drove Paul and his neighbours mad. And Paul admits he snuck out of his house to throw hot dogs at the box some nights when he thought no one was looking.

Paul's next job was to try and raise money as well as laughs by taking part in *Celebrity Driving School* for Comic Relief. He joined old pal Nadia Sawalha, soon-to-be pal Jade Goody and a group of others for some intensive lessons and a very public test. The 9 million viewers who tuned in confirmed that it all made great television. But Paul didn't exactly shine in the driving seat. 'He was by far the worst driver,' says producer Pip Banyard with a smile. 'He decided to learn in an automatic as he didn't understand gears so all he had to do was steer. But he couldn't even do that.' He could, however, complain loudly about everything that went wrong – and one of his mini-tantrums would ultimately be nominated for a *Best Television Moment Of The Year* award. Neither Paul nor any of the other celebrity learners passed their tests on screen, though Paul carried on with his lessons away from the cameras and got his licence four months later just before his forty-eighth birthday. As a double celebration he treated himself to a nippy little VW Beetle Cabriolet and says he should have got a car years ago.

But where was Lily all this time? Panto audiences in Manchester had seen her over Christmas. But as far as everyone else was concerned she was still in a bin liner in Paul's garage. And in 2003 that was where he intended she would stay. Paul, the care worker who had dominated the comedy circuit, sung on West End stages and become a gameshow favourite had discovered yet another new mountain to climb. Angela Clarke, the sister of *Letter to Brezhnev* and *The Good Sex Guide* star Margi Clarke, had just sent him a script to look at. Paul loved it. He was ready to star in his first proper sitcom.

CHAPTER TEN

Time For A Sitcom

Paul was sitting sweating in a cold rehearsal room in a west London church hall. It was the first read-through of the *Eyes Down* script and he was far more nervous than he had expected. It felt like the first day of school, he told friends that evening. Only with a lot more pressure and absolutely no chance of sneaking off home after lunch.

'Tell me if I'm doing anything wrong.' Paul looked around the room at the production team and the other actors. He was keenly aware that while he was due to be the star of the show they were the real professionals. 'The cast are proper actors, they have proper pedigrees. I'm just an old turn who used to dress up as a peroxide shoplifter and play the Vauxhall Tavern. Even on

Blankety Blank I would just turn up at 4pm, get a bit of slap on, do my stuff and go home. Now there's that thing called acting – and all the business of learning the scripts and rehearsals. It's terrifying.'

But *Daily Record* reporter Tim Randall, who spent several days watching Paul at work in that first week of rehearsals, remembers that the star did have a huge amount of faith in the project. He also had a pretty low opinion of the comedy competition.

'Have you seen *My Family*?' Oh please. It's like having teeth pulled,' Paul told Tim, rolling his eyes as he spoke. 'That's why until now I have always held out against doing a sitcom. They're all middle class shit and I don't really rate them. Anyway, the scripts I get for everything are always the same. I'm either a hard-bitten drag queen who says: "Take it from me, kid, life's tough", or I'm a drug addict or some old tranny. *Eyes Down* was just one of all those scripts I get to look at, but when I read it I just roared with laughter. I thought it could have been written especially for me. You know a script is good when you want to nick the material, which is what happened with this. Every line is a winner. After my heart attack I realised I had been making loads of money but had been miserable as sin at work. So I thought I would only do shows I liked.' And he liked *Eyes Down*.

Set in the down-at-heel Rio Bingo Hall on Merseyside, it was perfect Paul O'Grady territory, a cross between *Dinnerladies* and *Phoenix Nights*. Paul was playing Ray, the unpleasant, embittered manager and bingo caller who takes all his frustrations out on his colleagues and customers. He was a fantastic comedy monster – savage in nature, if not in name. 'I actually think he's related to Lily somewhere down the line,' Paul laughed. 'The two of them are tarred with the same evil brush. Ray hates humanity – pensioners in particular – but when you look at what he has got to deal with you're not surprised he's wicked and snide. He's a deeply frustrated man. He thinks he should be doing something better. He's been there eighteen years and he's had enough.'

As far as Paul was concerned, playing Ray was also both 'a challenge and a change'. His costume, hair and make-up sessions were a breeze compared to those of Lily, the Child Catcher, and the Wicked Queen in panto. And it was inspiring to be working with a whole new team of people again and learning some new skills. 'The transition from stand-up or live show to sitcom is littered with disappointments,' says Radio 4's television critic Charles Pierce. 'If you're going to get it right you do need to be open to new ways of projecting yourself. The timings are subtly different as well, and if you aren't flexible enough to take the new styles on board you won't be convincing in your new role.'

And Paul was desperate to get it right – because the more he rehearsed the more he loved his new role. 'All I've done today is laugh because I've got the most evil lines,' he told Tim Randall after one of the final *Eyes Down* rehearsals in west London. 'Ray is one of those people who say the things you would like to say but don't have the guts.'

But was Ray's character actually a little too close to Paul's for comfort? 'He's an evil, twisted man who hates everything that moves. Not exactly a challenge for me,' Paul conceded on a good day. But on other occasions he wanted to draw a line between them. 'Ultimately, Ray is a loser who hasn't got any mates. That's why he spends all his time in a bingo hall. So when people say they think I'm playing myself I'm like, Hang on a minute – are you having a go or what?'

Filming began in the late spring and early summer, and after the series was edited and polished up it won a prime BBC1 comedy slot at 9pm on Friday nights. But what would the critics think? High-profile new shows like this often have big screenings for the media, with strictly embargoed tapes sent out to those critics unable to attend. The writers then have up to a week to prepare their verdicts. For *Eyes Down* the producers say there were plenty of laughs in the screening room and a lot of smiling faces milling around the bar afterwards. But everyone knew this wouldn't necessarily translate into good reviews.

Unfortunately they were right. Several papers pretty much ignored the show. Others seemed to damn it with faint praise. Rupert Smith's comments in the *Guardian* summed it up. 'Paul O'Grady is without doubt the funniest stand-up comedian of the past twenty years and a proper star in the variety tradition,' he began. 'But whether or not Paul can be funny with a script is still a moot point and it is going to take more than the derivative dialogue of Angela Clarke's *Eyes Down* to settle the question.' In other papers Paul's own performance was described as 'Lily Savage-lite', while the rest of the show was deemed 'a sub-Victoria Wood mixture of vulgarity and bathos'.

Fortunately, audiences seemed to lap it up. The *Absolutely Fabulous* style of politically incorrect comedy was still at its height, and the pensioner-baiting and bad mouthing of *Eyes Down* allowed it to ride this wave with confidence. Key scenes were also singled out with awards nominations – not least the one where the staff are preparing the venue for a party.

'So, can you really not feel anything in your legs at all?' Ray asks the wild, wheelchair-bound Pamela, in what seems like a rare moment of kindness and empathy.

'No, I can't. Nothing at all,' she replies.

'Great. Then carry this,' he says, dumping a beer crate on her knees and using her as a human trolley for the rest of the episode.

Sometimes slapstick, sometimes farcical, sometimes bittersweet, the show retained its audience throughout the run. And as everyone waited to see if a second series would be commissioned, Paul was busy putting out feelers for other work. For a while there were rumours that he was going to get a cameo role as a long-lost member of the Dingle family in *Emmerdale*, and he was also offered a role on Gordon Ramsay's *Hell's Kitchen*. He turned this one down flat, partly because he hates the idea of being in a reality television show and party because he says the childhood boxer in him wouldn't have stayed hidden. 'I reckon I would have floored him within a day,' he told friends, effectively denying us what could have been the television moment of the year. There was also pressure for him to film more *Blankety Blank* episodes, even though Paul joked that the theme tune alone was now giving him nightmares.

The biggest story – which everyone was trying to keep secret – was that Paul was in line for a big money deal to revive another television dinosaur: *The Generation Game*.

The show had helped the BBC to dominate Saturday-night ratings throughout the 1970s and beyond, and had turned hosts Bruce Forsyth and Larry Grayson into the biggest stars of the day. In 2003, though, the BBC's Saturday night schedule had fallen well behind the Ant and Dec-dominated shows on ITV. The corporation needed a ratings winner. And it was prepared to spend nearly £1 million on two pilot shows to see if Paul could rustle one up with *The Generation Game*.

As it turned out, the attempts would end in acrimony, anger and a rare public failure. Paul sat in on production meetings over the course of nearly four months as everyone worked out how to bring the old show up to date. He then spent five hours in front of the live studio audience filming the first of the two planned pilots – suffering a neck injury in an accident on a spacehopper along the way. But for all the laughs, there were long stretches of silence as the audience shuffled in its seats, looked at their watches and wondered how long they would have to stay in the studio. Paul knew instinctively that something wasn't right with the show and the production team agreed with him. The problem was that no one could really identify what the problem was or who was to blame.

A war of words began in the trade papers and then made it to the nationals. The first pilot was said to be unusable and anonymous sources supposedly told reporters that Paul had been 'a square peg in a round hole' on the show. It was a claim Paul strenuously denied. 'I have been long enough in this game to know when I'm messing up and when someone else is,' he said ominously, as the post mortems continued. Even BBC1's Controller Lorraine Heggessey was drawn into the row when she admitted that it sometimes might take 'two or three goes' to get a new show right. Paul, though, didn't want to waste any more time on a project he felt was dead in the water. And he had already found another role to play – one which would ultimately lift his career to even greater heights. Ironically, it was in the medium he had derided so comprehensively during his convalescence the previous year. He was appearing on daytime television, filling in for Des O'Connor on *Today with Des and Mel* on ITV.

The show was great fun but relied hugely on the personalities of its presenters to keep viewers amused. Paul and Melanie Sykes had the right chemistry from the start and soon became close friends away from the cameras. And Paul surprised himself by loving the slightly manic air of a live daytime broadcast. That year he made a record nine appearances as guest host when Des was on holiday or otherwise engaged. And every one of them left him on a high. Perhaps he should do more of this, he thought.

In the meantime there was somewhere else he wanted to be – at his farm in Kent. His drivers sped him back there from the London Studios after his *Today with Des and Mel* shows were filmed. And as soon as he left London Paul started to relax. Country life didn't just appeal to him – he genuinely thought it might have saved his life. 'I've gone from the biggest drag queen in Soho to Farmer bloody Giles,' he joked to Mel after a show one day. 'I just rattle happily around the fields and it's incredibly therapeutic. If I've had a bad day I just go off for a walk. There's nobody to abuse but the cows and Dot my cow is well up for me if I do start yelling.'

He was also happy to report that he had dramatically cut down on the booze. When big groups of friends came for the weekend, they would still get roaring drunk and have a fantastic time. But their host was happy to stick to water. 'Then the next day they are all holding their heads and I've been up for hours. I've dug an allotment or something while they've been sleeping it off. It's fantastic.' What he was still struggling with were the cigarettes. He had smoked very few in the past two years but says the urge was still there from the moment he woke up to the moment he went back to bed.

At the National TV Awards with Fern Britton in October 2004.

Punk love-in with Sex Pistol Johnny Lydon at the British Comedy
Awards in December 2005.

Walkies for Buster and Paul.

Top: A Royal Variety Performance with Cilla, Elton and Her Majesty.

Bottom: Elton John was also a guest on Paul's own show in 2006.

Ten years at the top! Paul celebrates with a *TV Quick* award in September 2006.

In late September, 2006, Paul made a return to his chat show with his dog Olga.

Paul was a made an honorary fellow of Liverpool John Moores University.

Paul and Buster, together in October 2006.

'All those people who give up the cigs and say: I feel wonderful. My arse you feel wonderful. I would still kill for a ciggie and I will for the rest of my life.' So sometimes he admits he lapses. He might sneakily smoke a pack of twenty over the course of three or four stressful days. Not something he was proud of, but a far cry from the hard-partying, pre-heart attack times when he could need up to four packs to see him through a single day.

But any health damage Paul did by smoking the occasional cigarette was probably repaired by his incredible new diet. He was putting a huge amount of time and effort into growing organic food on his land – and every year he also harvested baking apples and plums from his orchards and spent days baking dozens of pies and crumbles to fill up his freezers and hand over to friends as gifts. Then there was the sloe gin, the chutneys and the pickled onions he made every autumn, while the radio blared out in his kitchen. 'Nobody can say the country is boring,' he says of his new routine, well aware that his former townie friends simply couldn't believe how domesticated he had become. But in truth he was simply reverting to type. The grubby little boy who had spent his summers playing in the peat bogs of Ireland had resurfaced in adult form. And he was still loving every minute of it.

Funnily enough, other elements of Paul's past were also resurfacing in the Kentish hills. The long-dormant social worker in him was coming to the fore as his menagerie of animals grew bigger – and stranger – by the day. The latest addition was a pet lamb, Waupie, who thought she was a dog and greeted visitors with a tiny wagging tail (and a lot of droppings on the kitchen floor). His new dove was just as much of a character. 'She's a trollop. She smashed her eggs, attacked her husband and went off with a wood-pigeon,' Paul laughed, appalled. Meanwhile, his favourite dogs Buster and Lewis were still creating havoc running around Dot's feet, while pigs Blanche and Jane would mooch around the fields with the chickens and the geese. Throw in the goats, donkeys, ducks and even the love birds that have nested with him over the years and Paul sometimes reckoned he was ready to build an ark.

'Ferrets, bats, mice, I've got them all. We could give the Osbournes a run for their money in this house,' he says of the animal magic that went on all around him. And still he wants more. He says he gets incredibly upset watching pet rescue programmes on television and has to stop himself from volunteering to re-house anything in need. 'I ring up and say: "I'll have that eagle. I'll give that polecat a good home." It's out of control.'

As a doting uncle and godfather to Amanda Mealing's sons, Milo and Otis, Paul admits his caring side extends to humans as well as animals – though he accepts that he is unlikely to get the chance to prove it. 'I've got a big house and if I could fill it with adopted kids I'd do it happily because I do have a strong nurturing side. But who would let me adopt? I'm forty-eight, gay, single and with a dicky heart,' he said with typical honesty.

What he didn't know was that his family was about to get a little bigger without any effort on his part. Daughter Sharyn and her boyfriend Philip were regular visitors to the Kent farmhouse and the group would often head off to the local pub in Aldington to chat the night away with the other regulars. Paul thoroughly approved of former boxer Philip and was thrilled at how happy his daughter seemed to be with him. And he was even more pleased when his phone rang one evening and Philip told him he was about to propose. It was an old-fashioned and lovely thing for a prospective son-in-law to do. And Paul admits that he cried after hanging up and telling Philip he wanted a full report as soon as he had popped the question.

When Sharyn called and said she had said 'Yes' straight away, Paul was in the mood for a celebration. After scouting around several local antique fairs for a few months he bought himself a classic arts and crafts sideboard as a memento. Paul O'Grady had indeed matured.

Lily Savage was exactly the same, however – if not worse. 'I'm coming to town and I'm going to be more evil than ever,' she said, as she prepared for 2003's panto season at the Bristol Hippodrome. The ever-professional Paul had been on top form when it came to getting bums on seats. He happily agreed to as many interviews as were required to promote the show and pulled on his wildly feathered black outfit for more than a dozen photo-calls. It worked and the panto was another sell-out.

After its final curtain calls Paul was back at the converted cinema in Rayners Lane, north west London, filming the second series of *Eyes Down*. He and the rest of the cast were thrilled to have been asked back for another six episodes to be broadcast in the autumn. In the middle of the run, Paul also hosted the year's British Soap Awards and proved he was still as good with hecklers as he had been two decades earlier in the south London clubs. 'Oh come on. You want nice – get Lorraine Kelly,' he yelled after being booed for one particularly close-to-the-line jibe about a fellow celeb.

But what were Paul's longer-term plans? The industry was abuzz with rumours of a big new role. Television gossips got wind that something big was afoot, but no one knew exactly what it was. One story had it that he was going to do a six-month stint in a new Stephen Sondheim musical in the West End – before taking the show to Broadway for a further six-month run. Then there was talk of a comedy film with Paul taking on four different roles, including Lily, her sister Vera, her late mother and, of course, himself.

Paul laughed at the most outlandish of the rumours – but he also carefully stoked up a few of them to keep his name in the headlines. As a performer he was acutely aware of the importance of surprise. And he knew he was going to be throwing a big one when he came clean. Loving every minute, he announced that he had signed up to become ITV's new face of daytime television. He was getting a wildly lucrative five-days-a-week teatime slot. And he was doing it under his own name and in his own way. His whole life was about to change yet again. And the world was going to have to get ready for *The Paul O'Grady Show.*

CHAPTER ELEVEN

Chat Wars

Paul's phone rang non-stop with journalists wanting to know more about the new teatime show when the news broke in autumn 2004. But he wasn't the only one the press wanted to talk to. His old friends Richard and Judy were under siege as well. They were the reigning monarchs of daytime television. They had given Paul one of his first big breaks by inviting Lily Savage on to the Liverpool set of *This Morning* all those years ago. So how did they feel about him muscling on to their turf now? And what would they do to stop him stealing their audience?

Other questions were being asked about Paul's suitability for such a broad teatime slot. Wasn't his humour just a little bit too adult for the late afternoon?

Could a man who had shouted down hecklers in pubs really connect with the housewives, pensioners and school kids who were probably used to slightly fluffier fare? The two top ITV bosses who had arranged Paul's deal were adamant they had the right man. 'Paul is one of the funniest people on television – he deserves to be on it far more than he is,' said the channel's controller of entertainment, Mark Wells. Head of daytime television Dianne Nelmes was equally certain that the channel had made the right choice – and having launched Richard and Judy's daytime careers she knew exactly what she was talking about.

Funnily enough, the one person who had needed the most persuading about his suitability for the new slot was Paul himself. 'I was still snotty about daytime television,' he said, thinking back to the awful shows he had sat through at home after his heart attack. 'I still thought it was all about DIY, mohair sweaters and "Here's a nice economical Christmas hamper for a family of four".' His own show would be different, he vowed. And he couldn't have been more right.

The first broadcast came from his beloved London Studios on the south bank of the Thames – and there wasn't a Christmas hamper in sight. Instead there was a glorious mix of seemingly unscripted banter, chat and slapstick humour. The show was unashamedly populist, a riotous, endearingly kitsch romp with no pretensions to be anything other than pure entertainment. In some ways it was pure vaudeville, the long-lost tradition that

Paul had always adored and at which he excelled. There were novelty acts, talking dogs, whistling goldfish, extraordinary stories. His audience laughed like drains at his anecdotes and were brought right into the heart of the show. Viewers were asked to film their own news stories – many of them ultimately turning into stars in their own right. The ten-year-old boy Paul sent out with camera crew to interview Al Pacino was a classic – especially when he admitted to the bemused actor that he had never even heard of *The Godfather*, let alone seen it.

Kids, grannies, mums and students loved it, and within weeks everyone knew they were watching pure television gold. 'It's an hour of fun and nonsense,' was how Paul described it. But in truth it was so much more. Yes, he was working largely without a script. But he always had a plan. He always knew how to mix the right ingredients to produce a show that surprised as well as entertained. He knew, also, how to mix in the laughter and the tears, bringing in appeals for lost dogs and sick children among competitions that really meant something. One week his prize-winners might get some money to buy a new dress for a big night out. Another, they might get the chance to take friends and family to a local restaurant. It was simple stuff. But it worked.

Five days a week Paul would stride towards the on-set desk, a selection of his own framed photographs and ornaments on the shelves behind him – there are plenty of others on another dresser, rarely seen on air, to his right. For the full hour the show would be physically as well as mentally draining. Seemingly unable to sit still, he would dart around the set, playing games, joining in, making mischief and having fun. What was also clear from the start was that his celebrity guests were always people he liked. While many rival chat shows only included people who had a specific book, film or programme to promote, Paul's included his old showbiz pals who just wanted to share a laugh on what had become the hottest sofa in town.

'I wouldn't say I was a good talk show host, because the guests don't get a word in edgeways with me,' Paul admits. But that wasn't the point. He was proving himself to be a raconteur, comedian, interviewer and showman all wrapped up in one wildly enthusiastic, likeable and utterly life-enhancing host.

'Of all the jobs I have ever had, this is my favourite,' Paul said, as the series reached the halfway point of its initial eight-week run. And he wasn't the only one smiling all day. His bosses Mark Wells and Dianne Nelmes were able to report far better than expected ratings. A huge word-of-mouth campaign meant that *The Paul O'Grady Show* was starting to rival the seemingly impregnable *The Weakest Link* on the BBC, as well as Richard and Judy's show on Channel 4. And it was then that things started to get ugly.

Looking back, it's hard to say if the supposed 'war of words' between Paul, Richard and Judy would ever have become so heated if it hadn't been for the tabloids. But with anonymous 'sources' and 'close friends' popping up with quotes almost every day, and the stars themselves being quoted and misquoted alongside them, the stage was set for what were soon dubbed the Chat Wars. Cushions were flying and it looked as if there could be blood on the sofa before it all ended.

The first salvos were fired as Richard and Judy continued to move their show upmarket, adding a wine club to the extraordinarily successful book club they had pioneered the previous year. People close to Paul allegedly laughed off the idea, saying it would turn off rather than attract new viewers.

Then came the battle for the best celebrity guests. Things came to a head when Joan Collins set out to promote her latest book, *Misfortune's Daughters*. She was booked to appear on Paul's show on 13 October before joining Richard and Judy a week later. But the papers screamed that *Richard & Judy*'s production team weren't happy. Joan was apparently told to cancel her appearance with Paul or face not just being banned from prime ITV slots herself, but seeing her fellow Random House authors getting the cold shoulder as well. Despite the fact she herself said how unfair it all seemed, Paul's 13 October show came and went without Joan's appearance. And he was furious.

'They're fighting dirty now,' Paul was quoted as saying the next day. 'I'm not bothered what's on the other side but they have said, If you come on my show you don't go on theirs for three years. How stupid is that?'

Before the dust had even settled, a new front in the

war had opened up. *Richard & Judy* claimed the coup of winning Madonna for a star interview. Paul refused to let it bother him. 'I don't give a toss who they've got. It could be the Pope for all I care. Whoever they get I'll still be nailing them in the ratings, day in and day out. No amount of publicity stunts can revive their show,' he declared. It was fighting talk but Paul was on relatively safe ground. He was winning between 2.5 and 2.7 million viewers a day, often at least half a million more than his big rivals on 4. Some days he was also beating *The Weakest Link*, sweet revenge on Anne Robinson, the other Merseysider in the year's extraordinary daytime ratings wars.

Feeling on top of the world Paul knew he could allow the spats and the arguments to wash over him. Yes, he famously says, he loves a good feud. But he also believes in fair play. So when he read one final report saying he had launched a 'furious attack' on Richard and Judy saying: 'They will be their usual snivelling, grovelling selves around Madonna,' he knew it was time to calm things down. The story had been pure fabrication. He had never thought those words, let alone said them. So he wrote to both the reporter and the paper concerned to get an apology – telling friends afterwards that he never got a reply from either. But he also sent a note and a big bunch of flowers to Richard and Judy.

'They are a lovely couple and we certainly haven't fallen out. I hate all the fuss that's being made. It's worse than the court of Queen Elizabeth I with all the bitching and intrigue. You'd think someone had invaded Poland for all the fuss this has caused. And it's like nothing else in the world matters any more except this supposed battle. I'll get an Oscar and all anyone will say is, "How do you think Richard and Judy will react?" It's ridiculous.'

Behind the scenes, Paul decided to let his work do his talking for him. If *Richard & Judy*'s big budgets and flash goody bags did allow them to scoop up more than their fair share of the big celebrity guests, then Paul and his team would simply think more laterally about how to respond. They would play to his show's light-hearted strengths and prove that there's more to entertainment than wheeling on a chart-topper or an Oscar-winner every few months.

So when *Richard & Judy* won a rare interview with Ringo Starr, Paul was simultaneously 'chatting' to a dancing collie. When they finally did the big interview with Madonna, he was introducing Mitzi Mueller, the 1970 Ladies World Wrestling Champion. 'They got Madonna and we got Mitzi,' he joked afterwards. But it was Paul and Mitzi who got the bigger audience.

In November the National Television Awards ceremony was a perfect place for the world to see if Paul, Richard and Judy really were back on speaking terms. Every famous face in the industry was there and most of them were straining to see how the teatime trio would act if they came face to face in the crowds. Anyone hoping for a bit of unscripted drama was disappointed. Back stage all three of them chatted calmly, and effectively buried the hatchet. Though Paul, of course, wanted the last word. Thinking back to the day four years before, when Judy had inadvertently flashed her bra at the same ceremony, he had some advice for her. 'Look love, even if you whip out both boobs live on air my show will trounce yours.'

'Paul is what you might call a very volatile person,' Judy told the *Independent*'s Ciar Byrne with a smile when they chatted about the spat a few weeks later. 'I think he says things without thinking and without realising what he has really said. But as far as we are concerned there is no way we are in a ratings war with him. Paul's supposed rivalry with us, whether he really feels like that or not, is just bonkers as far as we are concerned.'

Everyone was hoping that the teatime television market could actually be broad enough for all the big egos currently thrashing around in it. Audience figures showed Paul's arrival had actually attracted new viewers rather than just poaching existing audiences from the established players. So, as everyone got ready for their Christmas and New Year breaks, it felt as though it was all still to play for in 2005. And as far as Paul was concerned, the concept of a Christmas and New Year break didn't exactly apply.

It was panto time, *Snow White and the Seven Dwarfs* had finally made it to London and Paul was back as the ultimate killer queen. His bejewelled, bewigged and befeathered costumes were as outrageous as ever. But in

December 2004 nothing was quite as grand as his pay cheque. Insiders said Paul was earning a staggering basic salary of £70,000 a week. But when profit-related bonuses were included in the tally, Paul was expected to become the first panto star to earn a six-figure weekly sum. His Wicked Queen would be one of the most lucrative roles in theatre history – and it wasn't just actors who were looking on in envy. When the newspaper's Rich Lists were published in the New Year, they showed that Paul's panto money put him right up alongside premiership footballers in the earnings' stakes. In 2004, Roy Keane was marked as the best-paid player on £100,000 a week, while Wayne Rooney, the game's latest golden boy, had to get through the week on just £50,000.

Paul was to prove worth every penny though – in both financial and critical terms.

The money-men said that *Snow White* had taken more than £1 million in advance ticket sales before it opened. With the most expensive tickets costing £35, and 1,540 seats on offer at each performance, the producers were expected to see more than £600,000 a week pour into the Victoria Palace box office. Merchandising, drinks and refreshment sales would boost the total even further. Anyone who watched Paul in rehearsals or backstage had to agree that he worked hard for his share of the money. He dominated the stage and when he wasn't in view he was normally in the wings rushing through one of his extraordinary nineteen full costume changes. 'Thank God for Velcro,' he joked, as his dressers rushed to help him get ready for his next scene. Being Lily again (or at least being Lily being the Wicked Queen) was also great fun.

'It burns, it burns! What is it?'

'It's daylight, Your Majesty,' were the opening lines when the Wicked Queen first came into view. Lily was wearing dark glasses, suffering an almighty hangover and ready to let rip. Paul had always loved adding new topical references to the show he had co-written more than six years earlier. And this time he enjoyed having some bitter-sweet stuff among the jokes – in 2004 his Lily was clearly feeling her age and was obsessed with Botox, plastic surgery, collagen and miracle skincare routines. 'If it weren't for the tax bills I'd be in Barbados with Cilla,' he joked, a great line for the adults in the audience who might have missed the stories about his bumper earnings. And for the children, there was plenty of slapstick and pointed comments.

'What's that smell of poo, snot and old socks?'

'Why, children, of course,' Lily says, answering her own question a fraction of a second before the audience does it for her. But in her view, not every child is as smelly as the next. 'Don't you flick your impetigo down on the posh lot in the stalls,' she yells, pointing up to the kids in the cheap seats in the upper circles. There are more huge laughs when Lily lets fly at the mums, dads, social workers and probation officers she reckons are in the audience, and as usual she keeps up a running commentary on the production's supposed defects. 'It's a deathtrap,' she would say on cue as she tottered down the deliberately wobbly staircase halfway through the first act.

This being pantomime, there were also some dodgy song and dance numbers – as well as his favourite Edith Piaf. And Paul being Lily being Marlene Dietrich being a gypsy was one of the funniest and most complicated routines on stage that year. Finally, Lily transforms herself from bad queen to good with a backdrop of *Sound of Music* schmaltz, taking her curtain calls looking like a cross between Julie Andrews, Little Bo Peep and Grayson Perry.

While Paul was breaking box office records in west London, he was keenly aware that a rival pantomime just south of the river was winning more headlines. Of all people, Sir Ian McKellen had decided to throw theatrical caution to the wind and appear as Widow Twankey in the Old Vic's 'traditional' production of *Aladdin*. As he and his team updated their scripts for *Snow White*, Paul felt he had to have a dig at the thesps on the South Bank.

'But Snow White isn't ugly.'

'Oh yes she is!' yells Lily as the crowd rushes to join in.

'Oh no she's not!'

'Oh yes she is!'

'Oh no she's not!'

'Oh yes she is! And that's it. I'm only doing three of those. It's in my contract. If you want that kind of rubbish go to the Old Vic,' Lily barked every evening and matinee to prove she was on top of her game. The critics certainly agreed. In the battle of the panto dames, Paul was to win some extraordinary reviews from some of the most influential of critics. Benedict Nightingale of *The Times*, for example, is known as the doyenne of theatre writers. And he put Paul streets ahead of her Oscar-nominated rival at the Old Vic. 'Ian McKellen's Widow Twankey is as jubilantly over-the-top as his dresses, but Lily Savage depends less on the costume department and more on the sharp, knowing, streetwise quality of a comedian in instinctive contact with his or her audience,' he wrote. 'No one else on stage can compare with her,' declared John Gross in the *Sunday Telegraph*. 'This is a one-woman show, and it's not Snow White's. Lily was born to play the Wicked Queen, and when she's not on stage it's like someone has turned out the lights.'

Paul went back to Kent for his single day off in the holiday season. Nine family and friends came over to spend the day in the country and most joined their host at midnight mass in the village the night before. The farmhouse was warm and well decorated and Paul was loathe to leave it on Boxing Day, when he was whisked back to London for two more sell-out shows and their 38 costume changes.

Just over two weeks later, when the show's run ended and Lily's costumes and make-up were peeled off for the final time, Paul was uncertain what to do next. Life was so much easier when he could perform as himself and didn't have to dress up in sky-high wigs and inch-thick war paint. But panto had reminded him that there was still something magic about Lily. Job offers for her were still coming in regularly, though most were simply for game shows and guest appearances that left him slightly cold. Lily had started out as a rough act in tough pubs. Without the edge he got from that heritage, Paul felt as if he was cheating himself, his character and his audience. Lily would have to go back to the figurative bin liner in his garage. But maybe a live tour the following autumn would help drag her back out into the open. Before then he had to face up the fact that he hadn't yet crept out of Lily's shadow entirely.

'Oh look – that's Lily's dog! Do you walk her dog for her?' Two old ladies stopped Paul in the country lanes near his Kent farm early one January day that year. He decided to have a joke with them.

'Yes I do,' he replied.

'What's she like?'

'A right cow.'

'And they turned on me!' he told friends afterwards. 'How dare you! They said. She's given you a job and this is how you repay her. We're going to write to her. And they nearly hit me!'

The incident had kicked off because Paul's dog, Buster, had become one of the surprise stars of the first series of *The Paul O'Grady Show*. Buster had shaken himself and stood proudly on Paul's crowded desk several times a week. He had played up for the cameras some days, had ignored them completely on others. And he had brought some of the biggest laughs of the show. 'Funnily enough, what Buster also did was to give me a huge amount of new respect for Paul,' says fan Brenda Player. 'There was real love and care in the way Paul interacted with Buster. You got the feeling when you looked at them that he was a really nice man. It sounds stupid but there was something lovely and almost magical about the way they got on. It was a unique part of *The Paul O'Grady Show*, and a brilliant one.'

The second series began on schedule in the spring, with Paul now a central part of ITV's scheduling. Many of the station's other shows were going through some awful times so the top brass were thrilled that Paul was back to add a little buzz to their network. What they didn't know was that he was about to add some serious silverware to their awards' cabinets as well. The first shock came in March 2005, when *The Paul O'Grady Show* was named Best Daytime Programme by the Royal Television Society. The RTS is only now becoming better known to the general public, but it has always had huge credibility inside the industry and Paul said his award was a great personal honour. But an even bigger accolade was to come.

'And the Bafta for Best Entertainment Performance goes to .... Paul O'Grady for *The Paul O'Grady Show*!'

Paul sat stock still and silent as the crowd around him applauded and urged him to stand up and head for the stage. But for what felt like a lifetime he just couldn't move. Something inside told him to wait just a few seconds longer, to live in the moment and to savour this most wonderful of triumphs. 'It was the only time people have ever heard me be quiet,' he said afterwards, fully aware how unusual it was for a major Bafta to be given to a teatime show rather than a prime-time rival.

'I had always wanted to see what a Bafta looked like,' he joked at the post-show press conference, hardly able to take his eyes off the trophy now that it was his. But those who knew Paul well say there was something else troubling him that incredible night. There seemed to be a shadow hanging over him. A fear he couldn't quite push away. All his life, he says, he has run scared of tempting fate or getting too far ahead of himself. If he won £200 on the premium bonds he says he could confidently predict that the next envelope he opened would contain a £2,000 bill from the tax man.

However much went well in his life he always feared that something, somehow, would conspire to bring him right back down to earth.

'I'll pay for this,' he whispered to Cilla Black after collecting the Bafta from Davina McCall and arriving back at their table that night. It seemed, somehow, like too much good fortune. It seemed too good to be true. This wasn't a premium bond and the next letter might not contain a tax demand. But something told Paul that a new bill had just been run up. A new price would have to be paid. A shiver ran down his spine on what should have been the most triumphant night of his career. Someone had stepped across his grave.

CHAPTER TWELVE

The Greatest Loss

'Paul, what's this?' In his kitchen in Kent, Paul looked up. What the hell was Murphy on about now? What had he found, what was he joking about? But when Paul looked across the room his whole body froze. Somehow, he knew this wasn't a joke.

On the other side of the table Brendan was sitting pointing at a cup. An ordinary, common or garden teacup. And he didn't know what it was. He didn't recognise the object. Eerily calm, Paul tried to talk normally to the man who had shared and shaped his life for so long. But inside his mind was racing. This was the moment he had been dreading for the past decade. The one he had hoped would never come. 'Murph had come through liver cancer ten years ago and I had spent the time in between worrying whenever he coughed or had a headache,' Paul says. When cancer hits an organ as central to life as the liver, doctors say patients can never rely on total remission. So both Paul and Brendan were constantly aware that they could never truly relax. That was why they tried to live each moment to the full, to take on new challenges, go on new adventures and never worry about the consequences. One day, Paul had always feared, Brendan's cancer could come back. One day they might have to fight this awful illness one more time.

Paul walked the hospital corridors while Brendan had an MRI scan, biopsies and tests. He was a forty-nine-year-old man ready to care for the man he had always loved. But in his mind he was also the teenage boy waiting to hear if his mother would make it though the night. The same teenage boy who had seen his father die almost in front of his eyes. It was supposed to be spring outside but these were dark days in Kent.

They were also deeply frustrating. Delays and mix-ups seemed to be happening all around, with vital blood tests going missing and results taking too long to arrive. But eventually Paul and Brendan sat down with a consultant and heard the news they had both been dreading. Brendan's cancer had never fully disappeared – and now it had spread to his brain. Paul was told that Brendan could buy time with drugs that would reduce the swelling and the pressure on his brain. But the doctors said that the tumour itself would continue to grow. Surgery was out of the question and ultimately there was very little that anyone could do. But Paul refused to let Brendan go without a fight.

Back at the farm Paul realised he needed a nursing bed if he was to care for Brendan properly in his home. But none was available. A lady from one of the local hospices came round and told Paul she would order one but that it would take a few weeks to arrive. 'But we didn't have weeks,' Paul remembers, his voice a whisper. He felt, somehow, the urgency of Brendan's situation. The speed with which the days were passing. The dangers of letting go or giving up. 'We're not quitters, Murph,' Paul told him that day. And he would pull any strings to get the help they needed. Amanda Mealing, the friend who had shared so many good and bad times with both Paul and Brendan, was the person who found a way through the bed crisis. Of all places, she helped them to get one from the *Holby City* props department.

As Amanda, other friends and family all rallied round, Paul made a heat-wrenching decision. All he wanted was to spend every minute of every day with Brendan. But Brendan was adamant that *The Paul O'Grady Show* had to go on. He was its executive producer. He and Paul had worked so hard to win the slot and the profile. He wouldn't allow Paul to throw it away by opting out halfway through the crucial second season.

The other reason a pale and drawn Paul climbed silently into the back of the cars that drove him to London every day was that he wanted a complete news blackout on Brendan's illness. When the red lights for the cameras turned on, Paul wanted to switch on a smile and act as if it was business as usual. He would then continue with his usual production meetings by phone in the car on the way back to Kent. No one outside the pair's tight inner circle need know what was going on. It seemed the only way to ensure they got the privacy they needed, though the cost of living the lie was high. 'You have to hide it from people. You're not employed to go on TV and say, "I've had no sleep. Murphy's dying. I don't know how much longer he's got and I'm having terrible trouble with the doctors." You can't do any of that nonsense. You have to get on with the show,' Paul said. But every day it felt harder than the one before.

As Brendan's health deteriorated, the only thing that really helped, somehow, was the fact that Paul always knew he would be watching the live shows on the television beside his bed. The man who had always been there, at every performance Paul had ever done, would still be there in spirit. And Paul wanted to let him know that he was thinking of him. He tried to crack particular jokes, to say certain things and to send secret coded messages that he knew only Brendan would be able to decipher.

Back in Kent after each day's filming, the entertaining didn't stop. Paul would do everything he could think of to lift Murphy's spirits. He remembers tap dancing, playing the trumpet, doing whatever it took to get a smile. Years later, what makes him cry is the memory that even the dogs seemed to know something terrible was happening. Buster, in particular, would race up the stairs to be with his other daddy as soon as he returned from London. He would lie beneath Murphy's bed, keeping watch over him and trying to give whatever comfort he could. Everything, absolutely everything in those awful days made Paul want to cry. But he had to hold it all inside.

Once a care worker, always a care worker. Paul vowed that he alone would wash Brendan and help him with the toilet. But as Murphy got weaker and felt heavier, Paul admits he struggled with the lifting, though he refused to give in and still refuses to feel self-pity. 'It was really rough.' Four words. That's all he will say of the worst of those days when he fought to keep his partner's dignity intact. What also took Paul to the edge of tears so often that year were the simple acts of human kindness from so many people around him. He remembers in particular the neighbours from the village who closed ranks and refused to speak to the media about Brendan's illness – but who came round almost daily to offer help with the laundry, to look after the garden or to make meals when they knew Paul was too exhausted to do so himself.

As well as Amanda Mealing and her family, Cilla Black, Barbara Windsor, Gaby Roslin, Sue Johnston, Elton John and all the staff of *The Paul O'Grady Show* were wonderful too, he says in a whisper. All seemed somehow to know when to step forward and offer help and when to step back and give him space. Small, cleverly chosen gifts, such as packets of his favourite

Iced VoVos biscuits from Australia being left on the back seat of his car, gave him a reason to smile and meant a huge amount. Simple, practical assistance or time at the end of a phone counted for more than anything money could buy. 'None of my friends can ever be thanked quite enough,' Paul says.

In May, unable to sleep and desperate to relax, Paul crept downstairs in the early hours and started pacing around his house. He lit a cigarette early one morning. Then another. And another. Falling into his old chain-smoking habits didn't seem to matter one bit. He also stopped eating some days, and forced himself to go through the motions on others. And every day he had another mask to pull on at work, another role to play.

With Brendan's health deteriorating further and faster, Paul knew he had to act tough, even when he felt like falling apart. 'Right, enough moping around. We need to do this, and this, and this.' He was in full, business-like sergeant major mode, trying to focus on all the small things that would get them through their days. But nothing and no one could stop Brendan having a stroke as his cancer dug ever deeper into his brain. Afterwards, his mind could be as active as ever. But he could no longer talk. And like Paul he had always been a talker. 'It was like he was stuck behind a mirror,' Paul remembers. And it was awful. 'To watch someone you love, a healthy, eloquent man, unable to speak or walk is hideous.'

What made it all seem so much worse was that Paul's

50th birthday was approaching fast – a day that he and Brendan had planned to celebrate with a blow-out party for all their family and friends. The Kent farmhouse was supposed to be filled with music, laughter and joy that day. But what would they do now?

At first, the pair decided to simply scale down the celebrations but to still invite people round to cheer them both up. Their very nearest and dearest, those who had supported them so much in the past few months would be the ones to share the day. But when Brendan's health took another turn for the worse, they agreed that the whole event had to be scrapped. It would be too distracting, too hard for everyone. No invitations were sent out and just 48 hours before the big day Brendan would lose his battle for life. He had been taken in to Charing Cross hospital in London for radiation treatment, but had slipped away before it could be given. 'Go on, Murph. You can go now. We're all here and you don't need to hang on. I'll see you later.'

Those were the last words Paul said to the man who had shared so much of his life and helped him live so many of his dreams. It was a peaceful and dignified moment. Brendan was just 49 years old.

Wild flowers from Paul's farm filled the twelfth-century Kent church where Brendan's funeral was held. Paul had been inside the building early in the morning, cleaning the already spotless interior before the service because he felt that everything had to be perfect. Brendan was then buried in the churchyard outside. It was where Paul had told Murphy that he himself wanted to be buried. It had never occurred to either of them that Murphy would be the first to go.

Until this point, Paul says, he had hardly shed a single tear – and never once in public. It was his long-forgotten training as a social worker, his ability to build a distance between himself and the person he was caring for, that had seen him through. So too did the memories of his dear Aunt Chrissie, the woman he describes as 'one of life's copers', the kind who get on with things and keep their lives together when all around them seems bleak and broken. He drew on strength from family, friends, neighbours and strangers.

And then, after the funeral, when Brendan was finally gone, Paul went home to cry. He didn't stop for three days.

'Don't give in, don't give up.' That was the message Brendan himself had been giving him throughout their lives together. But it was tough, so very tough that summer. Paul lost two and a half stone, whole handfuls of his hair came out when he tugged it, and when he passed his hall mirror he saw a hunched-up old man he barely recognised shuffling past.

The doctors said he should take tablets to help him sleep and lift his mood. But he refused. He didn't want to mask his feelings or try to block out his problems. Professional grief therapy was also offered and politely refused. He could talk to his friends. It might be hard for them. It might be too difficult. It might even be boring.

But if they are true mates they will listen. He was right. Deep down he also knew that he could get through these awful, empty days. He could survive these terrible, endless nights. He vowed to carry on building the company that he and Brendan had formed. He would carry on making the shows they had loved. He would keep his wonderful memory alive.

CHAPTER THIRTEEN

Back in Business

The days felt too long in the hot summer of 2005 after Murphy's death. There was too much time, too many memories, too many tears. So when the crying finally stopped Paul did the only thing he knew that would stop him from falling apart. He threw himself into his work and into a frenzy of travel, friendship and activity.

He also walked right into a wall of criticism from those who barely knew him. Several people, he says, told him they couldn't believe how quickly he seemed to have moved on. How hard he seemed. But what they didn't know was that Paul was still in shock. He was back in the London Television Studios filming *The Paul O'Grady Show* as normal that September. But, he says, it would take him almost a year before it really sunk in that

Murphy was gone. It would take him almost a year to realise that his home in Kent would always feel empty. It would take him almost a year to cope fully with his loss.

'You're just dead inside. Nobody to please, nobody to entertain. You just feel alone,' he said quietly. He also felt torn and guilty whenever good fortune smiled on him. Ironically enough, 2005 was to be the year Paul won more acclaim than ever before: he and the show he had created with Murphy would collect gongs at the Baftas, the British Comedy awards, the National Television Awards, the Royal Television Society Awards and the TV Quick and TV Choice awards – among a host of other lower-profile ceremonies.

But Paul struggled to enjoy all the attention. 'It's fabulous to win but then you remember that the one person you feel you can really celebrate with isn't around,' he said, soberly, after collecting his RTS gong. But that said, he didn't disappoint his fans or run shy of getting some extra mileage out of his successes. The day after the Comedy Awards ceremony, for example, he walked on to the set of *The Paul O'Grady Show* with the award in a carrier bag.

At some of the other big awards shows he was also ready with a joke or a good line for the reporters on the red carpets outside. The night of the National Television Awards at the Royal Albert Hall was a good example. Paul walked up the red carpet with Buster under his arm – but had to then hand him over to a minder before heading into the hall itself. Some 140 years ago a rule had been made banning live animals from the venue. 'Buster, the star of my show, is so annoyed he can't come in,' Paul told reporters with a smile, as he kissed Buster's gorgeous head and saw him carried away. As it turned out, Paul would have one more reason for trying to keep smiling that first summer and autumn he spent without Murphy – because he was about to embark upon one of the most challenging and controversial periods of his life.

The first storm broke in August – and it was potentially career threatening. Paul had been advertising for new young roving reporters to join the show. It didn't matter who you were, what you did or where you lived – if you had the Paul O'Grady spark, then you stood a change of being selected. Or so everyone thought.

Mum Nina Chaplin was one of the many people to see the initial advert and her daughter Megan, eight, was one of the thousands to apply. Megan was interviewed by phone and after a few weeks Nina rang the producers to see whether her daughter was being considered for the role. The producers said they would email her – but someone pressed the wrong button and Nina was sent the notes that the team had made on around 650 applicants – including Megan herself. It made horrific reading. Alongside everyone's names and addresses were some terse, tough comments. 'A bit of a psycho', was the verdict on one viewer. An eleven-year-old girl was damned as 'nerdy-looking' while a thirteen-year-old had 'common and thick' against her name. 'Black girl: NO' said another, the capital letters making a bad comment even worse. 'I think he is special needs.' 'Lesbian – no.' The shameful list went on and on...

'I loved the show, but all my love and respect for it has gone. I won't be watching again,' said one of the most criticised viewers when the papers got hold of the dossier and called her up. The others – all of whose contact details were suddenly in the papers' hands – were equally upset. And so too was Paul. He was on a week's holiday when the crisis first broke. But when he returned he took charge and demanded immediate action. One of his production team was sacked and another suspended. This must never happen again, he said – and he meant it. 'The comments about children trying to get on to the show were appalling. I would like to say sorry to anyone who was upset and offended. I will not tolerate this behaviour; it is totally unacceptable. There is no place for anyone working on my show who makes comments like this.' Paul sent flowers and personal messages to those worst affected in the scandal. But it would take some time to win round the viewers.

'I would never have let my daughters audition if I had known what staff were saying behind their backs,' one mum told the papers as the storm rumbled on. 'It's so mean. They shouldn't have asked us along if they just want to laugh at us,' said one of the humiliated youngsters, who was almost in tears as she spoke about her shock. The saddest thing about the scandal was that no one could ever have been nicer to his audience members than Paul. He loved his roving reporters and real-life commentators. The people given cameras and told to seek out stories and have fun for him had become a huge and successful part of his show. Their faces and life histories were on his website and some were already being launched as stars in their own right because of the breaks Paul had given them. So to suddenly be seen as a showbiz monster who didn't give two hoots for his viewers' feelings was an awful situation for Paul to be in. And that's why he was so determined to put the jibes behind him and find a new and more positive way to select his next generation of on-screen helpers.

Christmas that year was a sober affair. As usual, Paul tried to fill his Kent farmhouse with friends and family. But without Murphy there would always be something missing. And as winter gave way to spring, Paul had one date looming large in his diary. If he had lived it would have been Murphy's 50th birthday and Paul spent that day alone, his mobile turned off, in the graveyard where he had been buried. Year after year that had been how his mother had spent his father's birthday – and now he was in the same boat Paul knew exactly why she had done it. It wasn't about keeping up appearances, he said. It was to feel close to the person you miss more than anything. And to keep their memory alive in your heart. Passing this milestone was a big achievement for Paul. And after holding things inside for so long he finally felt able to talk more publicly about the man who had spent so long in the shadows, but who had been so important to his life.

'Murphy was quite fiery but he was the oil on my water – the calming influence. There were fireworks at times but that's what made the relationship so strong and such fun. Murph and I were like brothers, joined at the hip, thick as thieves. It transcended any sexual relationship we'd had. This was a partnership. A double act. Emma Peel and John Steed. Laurel and Hardy,' Paul told his old pal Sue Carroll.

Paul says that as the weeks, months and ultimately the years pass, he no longer feels he has to rush home from the television studios to cry. But he did still spend so much of his time just wondering where his partner in crime had gone, and missing him with all his heart. 'It's not about me; it's about him. You miss them so much, you think, "Where the bloody hell are you?" So yes, I get lonely. It's a real melancholy. You just keep thinking, "Oh bugger, it's not fair." I bought a Mini recently and thought, "Oh, Murphy would love this." But he's not here. It's this constant regret...' Paul's words fade away, his rasping Liverpool voice deeper and more muffled than it ever is on stage.

Melancholy and regret are not Paul's natural states, however. And flashes of anger would often replace them in those grim days. 'Why him and not me?' Paul would rail at the skies as he paced around his farm. 'I've been the one who's had the heart attack, who has been at death's door. Murphy was a young man still. He should be living, enjoying himself. It's not right. I'd give everything I have for Murphy to be on holiday and not lying in that grave.'

So was there a purpose to it all? Was there a reason why Paul had been spared and Murphy had been taken? Sometimes he felt that there must be. And so he vowed to make the most of all the time he himself had left – and to take up the fight on behalf of one particular group of people he admired more than almost anyone else: carers. These were the people he had worked with as a social worker what seemed like a whole lifetime ago. They are the people who look after the ill day in and day out, year after year, with minimal support or relief.

'Yes, I keep banging on about carers,' he would say in the production offices and in newspaper interviews, after mentioning them yet again on one of his shows. 'But if I don't, then who will? All the parents with disabled and sick kids. All those old ladies who have quietly nursed dying husbands for years with no one to talk to.' There is a mix of sadness and anger in Paul's voice as he speaks of them. An unshakable belief that more has to be done to recognise the sacrifices they make and the burdens they endure. Fronting up the Community Service Volunteers' Get Active Week that year was one high-profile and practical way to do it. But he promised to do plenty more behind the scenes for as long as he was able.

Fortunately for Paul's peace of mind, his tempestuous, passionate Liverpool upbringing had taught him that good times can always mix with the bad. The sailors' wives had proved to him that great joy can come amid deep tragedy. So he never felt he was betraying Murphy's memory by smiling, laughing or looking forward to things. And suddenly there was much to be happy about.

The first surprise came when Liverpool John Moores University got in touch, saying they thought one of the city's most famous sons should be taken into the academic fold. He was offered honorary fellowship – a 'Bachelor of Tarts,' as Paul reckoned Lily would have joked. Wearing a purple trimmed gown and mortar board for the ceremony, Paul was in his element – and when he made his speech he was back at the top of his game.

'God will always protect you, but carry a brick in your handbag just to be sure. And my advice to you all? Don't nick anything you can't sell on and don't mix cider with Pernod.' It might not have been the most academic of announcements. But the students loved it and Paul nearly fell over laughing when he was also handed a specially made gown and mortar board for Buster to wear on the next show.

Shortly afterwards, Paul headed back to Liverpool for another event he had never expected to experience. He would be walking his daughter down the aisle. Sharyn was in a very pale pink wedding dress while Paul was in a Gieves & Hawkes morning suit. Everyone was smiling from ear to ear.

'Wonderful, just wonderful,' he says of his feelings that day. 'Sharyn looked so beautiful and vulnerable.' The ceremony at Liverpool Town Hall was simple and the reception riotous. 'Ask me what I'm proudest of in my whole life and I'll say: "Our Sharyn,"' he told the rest of the family that day as the drinks flowed and the dancing began.

Back in London, he admitted he was even starting to come round to the idea of one day becoming a grandfather. And love was still in the air – Paul had received an invitation to one of the highest-profile weddings of the year. It was the civil partnership between Elton John and long-time partner David Furnish. Paul had been picked as the compère at their celebrity-studded joint stag do. He introduced performers from Bryan Adams to the Pet Shop Boys and was ready for one hell of a party. 'I'm going to tie them to a lamp-post and cover them with shaving foam. It's the old-fashioned thing to do,' he joked with the armies of reporters camped outside the venue beforehand.

Back in his office at home, Paul had more serious plans afoot for the year ahead. Losing Brendan had made him even more aware of the speed at which time was passing. He had achieved so many of his goals so far – indeed he had surpassed most of them. But what of those that were still dangling just outside of reach? Should he sit back and forget them, or should he make one last lunge, before it was too late? None of his friends had any doubts that Paul would make the jump. Sitting back simply wasn't in his DNA. He had climbed so many mountains already. He wasn't going to stop now.

The problem was that his latest challenge involved business affairs, the one part of their joint world that Murphy had controlled and Paul had largely ignored. For years Murphy had said the pair should use their own production company to produce Paul's shows. The idea wasn't just to make more money – it was to have total control over every aspect of their joint destinies. And while Paul was always happiest on the shop floor – he says he loves bitching about the bosses and planning sneaky tea breaks with his colleagues – he could also see the attraction of becoming a manager. But did he want to do it on his own? The more he agonised about it, the more he realised he had to give it a try. This had been Murphy's big dream and Paul felt he owed it to him to turn it into reality. What he didn't know was how much trouble this decision would ultimately cause. Or that it would unleash a storm of criticism that would see Paul attract the very worst reviews of his career.

CHAPTER FOURTEEN
The Backlash

It was a crisp January day in 2006 when Paul climbed out of his car and looked up at the magnificent country house where he was joining some of the most powerful figures in the media world. They were planning a brainstorm of a lunch and there was plenty to discuss. Lord Waheed Alli was at the head of the table, the Labour peer who had increasingly been looking after Paul's business affairs since Murphy's death. Also there was Waheed's partner Charlie Parsons, one of the founders of *Big Breakfast* production company Planet 24 and an old friend of both Paul and Brendan. Channel 4's head of entertainment and comedy, Andy Newman, was also at the table, along with various other power players from the television and business worlds.

A big topic under discussion was ITV's refusal to let Paul keep his promise to Murphy and produce his own show. The channel wanted to carry on doing the job in-house. So the new company Paul had set up – Olga TV, named after his latest dog – was left without its key role. Further complications were also building up behind the scenes. Paul's contract was up for renewal and Simon Shaps had been appointed the new Director of Television at ITV. Rumours abounded as to everyone's intentions, so there was no shortage of conversation around Lord Alli's table that day. And there were some surprising suggestions as well.

'Why don't you join Channel 4?' someone said.

Once the question had been asked, Paul was unable to put it out of his mind. A fresh start might be just what he needed. It could buy him the control he craved. And the new challenges he thrived on. There are two problems, he told his fellow lunch guests that day in Kent. One was called Richard, the other was called Judy. How would *The Paul O'Grady Show* fit into the Channel 4 schedule? He could hardly work there while his old pals and rivals were the big stars. Or could he?

As the conversation became increasingly serious, Paul realised that Channel 4 might be big enough for everyone after all. If Richard and Judy took a bit more time off – something they had long since wanted – then there were enough weeks in the year for both the shows to shine. It would be like a television timeshare and as far as Paul was concerned it would be incredibly lucrative. An offer estimated at £2 million a year was put on the table. It would make Paul one of the best-paid stars in television – and his new contract would only apply to daytime shows. He would be free to make any number of prime-time programmes for rival channels.

'These kinds of deals don't come around very often. Paul's was an indication of how hot he was at that point and he would have been a fool not to take advantage of it,' says media lawyer Kevin Sainsbury. And Paul has never been a fool. So he made his decision. He would say goodbye ITV, hello Channel 4. And not surprisingly, Simon Shaps and his ITV execs were furious.

Ironically enough, a confidential research paper had been presented to the ITV bosses the day before Paul made his announcement. It said that he was the principal reason why the 5-6pm weekday slot was the only one across the whole of ITV to show year-on-year audience gains. Richard Hammond, whose show *Richard Hammond's 5 O'Clock Show* had been in the same slot in Paul's off-season, was attracting only half his audiences. And with so many other ITV shows doing badly – *Celebrity Wrestling* and *Celebrity Love Island* two key examples – the executives could ill afford to lose their one blue-chip star. A massive post-mortem was carried out and there were false rumours that Paul had actually left because of a clerical error: it was claimed that someone had forgotten to send out his updated contract. And that Paul had jumped ship because the oversight made him feel unwanted.

The reality was that Paul was simply looking for new challenges. He threw himself into the production meetings that would decide on the look, feel and content of the new show. Everything would be freshened up, but the overall programme would be the same relaxed and sometimes riotous mix. Even the name would hardly change – *The New Paul O'Grady Show* was picked. It does what it says on the tin, Channel 4 bosses said happily when they were told. But before the end-of-March date for the start of the new series a whole host of extra hurdles had to be overcome. First, and most important, came the venue for the new show.

Paul wanted to carry on filming at the London Studios. It was where so many of his past triumphs had taken place, right back to his Lily Savage days. After filming more than 170 *Paul O'Grady Shows* there, plenty of the production and behind-the-scenes staff had become good friends, and the main studio felt big enough to create plenty of atmosphere, yet small enough to allow plenty of contact with the audience. Unfortunately, ITV has a stranglehold on the venue, on the south bank of the Thames near the National Theatre. And to Paul's fury it refused to let him use it any more. Suddenly homeless and with the new series due to start in a matter of weeks, the production team started to panic. They needed a studio big enough for such a high-profile show, and available five days a week – and that didn't give them many options. Finally they got lucky – when they approached the BBC. 'The world is full of ironies,' Channel 4 boss Kevin Lygo said of Paul's enforced return to Studio 1 at Broadcasting House after so many years away.

The next problem came from an entirely unexpected source. It was the battle of Buster the dog. The previous year Granada had commissioned a firm of puppet makers to produce 5,000 nodding Busters to give away as prizes on Paul's original ITV show. The models were hugely popular and second-hand examples had started to sell for more than £200 each on eBay. Paul Louden, owner of the BlueSky factory that made the models, says fans were desperate to get hold of them from the start. 'Paul's fans tracked us down over the internet and the phones just went crazy. We had thousands of people calling up wanting to buy one at any price. People were literally begging to get their hands on a Buster for presents.' But everyone looked set to be disappointed, because ITV refused to allow BlueSky to make any more when their star jumped ship to Channel 4. It owned the Buster mould, it said, and it wasn't going to give it up.

As the Battle for Buster hit the headlines, anonymous sources from ITV spoke to the papers, and showed how bitter ITV was about the whole affair. 'Buster was the real star of the show and the general feeling is that we want to hang on to his image rights. We commissioned the Buster models to be made as prizes for the show and they've proved to be a big hit. Why should Paul get to cash in on something that was our idea in the first place?'

And if Paul had expected channel hopping to be easy, he got a huge shock on the morning of Sunday 26 February when he sat in Kent reading the tabloids. One of the papers – the *Sunday Mirror* – seemed to have declared open season on him. It was focusing on the rows over the location of his new show. And its comments were spectacularly harsh. Like so many other successful people, Paul was discovering that the higher you rise, the harder you sometimes fall. It was what the Americans call Tall Poppy syndrome – the desire to cut down those who are seen to have got above themselves. It was a bitter, unpleasant and unnecessary fact of showbusiness life. And that Sunday, Paul was finding out about it the hard way.

'Let's get this right. O'Grady completely shat all over the people who made him a chat show star by quitting his show – without warning – to go to Channel 4, who had offered him shed-loads of money,' began soon-to-be *Celebrity Big Brother* contestant Carole Malone. 'He did this without one jot of consideration or one shred of loyalty to those people who'd worked like dogs to make him a star and who were now up you know who's creek because this selfish madam had left them with a gaping hole in their schedules.' And she didn't stop there.

'After all that, O'Grady then has the brass neck to ask the same people he'd so spectacularly shat on if he could use their state-of-the-art studios so he can make a hit show for Channel 4. Obviously they told him where to stuff his request, which is why he has had a hissy fit. "I'd rather sweep the streets than work for ITV," says the big girl's blouse. If his Channel 4 show flops, that's exactly what he'll be doing.'

Shell-shocked and hurt, the still-grieving Paul couldn't find any consolation in other papers. That weekend another batch of unnamed 'sources' at ITV were being quoted elsewhere with various unflattering things to say about the man they had been praising as a ratings-winner just twelve months before. 'Very mercurial, we did well to hang on to him for as long as we did,' one of them allegedly told the business staff of *The Times*, when the paper examined the effect his defection might have on the channel's finances. 'A loose cannon. More trouble than he was worth,' said another as the onslaught continued.

The only good news that Paul could find as he headed back to the production offices the following day was that Richard and Judy were finally on his side. 'We're old mates of Paul's and his new job is terrific news. It's great not to be on rival channels and not to have to trade punches with each other any more,' said Richard. Judy added that the couple were thrilled that Paul's arrival would give them a few more weeks' holiday each year – something they clearly deserved after nearly twenty years in the daytime spotlight.

The trio also had a fun day out together when Channel 4 asked them to join the likes of Des Lynam and Noel Edmonds on a promotional photo-shoot – though in the fevered atmosphere of early 2006 even this would almost end in tears, with Paul forced to step in and defend his teatime colleagues. The problem arose the following week, when Des was chatting to the audience just before a *Countdown* episode was recorded. He told a series of funny stories about the photo-shoot and at one point he joked that Richard and Judy were no longer speaking to each other. Someone in his audience took the joke seriously, called the papers and a whole raft of new rumours began about the couple's relationship.

To his credit, Paul was one of the first to try and calm things down – happily making a joke at his own expense in the process. 'Richard and Judy are just fine. I just think Des was having a laugh. I know what I'm like with my audience before we go on air. The amount of times I've got myself in trouble. I'd come on and joke, "Bring me my drugs." It's a joke and you don't expect it to ever get taken seriously or reported.'

For their part, Richard and Judy were too relaxed to care about the latest rumours – they were getting ready to enjoy some time off. Their latest series was in its final week. In five days' time Paul's new show was set to start and at last he was feeling ready for it. 'We've had all the talk and the rowing. Now I just want to get on with it. I can't wait,' he told reporters at the press launch. He was also as wide-eyed as ever about his likely first guests – which was one reason why his audiences loved him. 'I still get star struck all the time. I couldn't believe meeting Ken Barlow – or should I say Bill Roache – and as for Jean Marsh from *Upstairs*,

Downstairs – words fail me, and that doesn't happen very often,' he laughed.

The following Monday, as the recording time approached, the producers were in for their usual nervous moments because Paul was still refusing to use a script and an autocue. 'I don't have a clue what I'm going to say before the programme starts because I think that gives you an edge,' is how he sees it. 'I treat the show as if I'm having a chat with someone.' And it's his show, he says. It can't be run by someone in a production gallery barking instructions into the presenter's earpiece. Paul had coped just fine standing on a crate in the corner of a dingy pub what felt like a thousand midnights ago. He would cope now, standing on stage in the west London television studios in front of some 200 lively fans.

As far as the critics were concerned the host had lost none of his old magic. 'What Paul has shown is that a single personality, honestly presented and blessed with comedy, can entertain the nation for an hour every day, every week,' wrote James O'Brien in the *Guardian*. Elsewhere, Paul was being touted as the British David Letterman – the American chat show host who everyone from Jonathan Ross down saw as the best in the business. And still the praise continued. 'There is no one to touch O'Grady for his quickness of wit, charm and ability to communicate with people of all ages,' wrote the chief television critic of *The Times*.

Sitting in the back of his car being driven back to

Kent, Paul couldn't entirely relax, however. His decision to set up his own company and jump channels was still having repercussions, and the backlash against him was still rumbling away beneath the surface. So, in his weaker moments, he still had some regrets. 'It's like being a small child in the middle of a very nasty custody battle,' he told friends as ITV and Channel 4 continued to slug it out in public and in private. The previous week he had been shocked when ITV tried to burst his relaunch bubble by repeating his old shows at 5pm, presumably to try and confuse viewers and draw them away from the new production. 'It's a hoot. All I need to do now is to piss the BBC off and get them to repeat *The Lily Savage Show* at 5 and I'll have world domination,' he said, trying to make light of it. 'I am not a repeat, I am live, this is the real me,' he joked on his new show to get the message across. More seriously, it was all looking a little ridiculous because the old ITV shows were so out of date – with soap stars talking about long gone storylines and viewers being asked to ring in for long-finished competitions.

What ITV didn't know was that these old shows were actually causing Paul a huge amount of pain. They were the shows he had filmed while Murphy was dying in bed at his home in Kent. They were the shows that included all the in-jokes, the hidden gestures and the secret signals that Paul had devised to let his partner know he was always in his thoughts. To have them aired again, less than a year later, was awful. Paul's memories of those terrible days were still too raw. The reminders were just too sharp.

Striding out across his fields in Kent that weekend he decided it was time to end this war with his former employer. In his anger at the money men and the faceless executives who seemed to be orchestrating the battle, he knew he risked hurting all the ordinary employees he had got on so well with the previous year. Many of these ITV staff had become friends. All had been wonderful in the low months, when Murphy was fading away and Paul had needed extra support. He didn't want any of them to think he was ungrateful. I love nothing more than a good feud, he had always said. But he didn't hold grudges. It was time to move on.

Back at work, Paul was throwing himself into the new show with abandon – often literally so. The humour was as slapstick as ever, including everything from fire eating and fireworks to bizarre exercise routines and full-on custard pie fights. The music was good, his guest list was still stellar, and everyone seemed to have a ball as they sat on his sofa then stood up to take part in whatever ridiculous game had been set up for the day. The Organ Game (which had been Guess The Tune on ITV) was still working well, Paul's roving reporters were also on good form, his competition entrants could make hilarious listening and a real community feel was building up around the show. Paul himself was also as instinctively funny as ever. 'Trinny and Susannah? I'd like to see those two in something long and flowing. The Thames,' he said during one show when the fashion gurus were mentioned.

'My hair could turn the same colour as yours,' Vernon Kay said to him, talking about the effect of extreme shocks.

'What do you mean? Brown?' asked Paul, throwing an arch look at the audience as he stroked his entirely grey locks.

'I started my career as a dancer,' began old pal Amanda Mealing on another show.

'Yes, with a pole,' Paul interrupted, as the studio fell about laughing.

But for all the fun and games there were still battles to be fought behind the scenes. One of them came when Channel 4 decided it had to make the *Find A Dog A Home* appeals self-supporting by introducing a ten-pence-a-call information line for viewers. Paul was adamantly opposed to it. On ITV, when the calls had been free, around 300 viewers a day had been calling the likes of The Dogs Trust and Battersea Dogs' Home after each show. More than twenty dogs had been found new owners in the process. But the Channel 4 charges saw the number of callers fall by an astonishing 90 per cent. And as the change happened just as it was announced that the latest series of *The X Factor* had been generating up to £350,000 a night out of its phone votes, it was easy to see why people would think Paul's show was profiteering. 'We need to go back to the way it was,' Paul told the Channel 4 executives. And he won the battle. His rag bag of tragic, adorable or just plain stupid dogs were soon back on the show with call charges removed. The Dogs Trust and Battersea Dogs' Home were happy to continue trying to find them new owners.

Holding an hour-long show together five days a week is tough enough. Doing so while you run a brand new production company adds an enormous amount of extra pressure. 'Where are you, Murphy, now that I need you?' Paul asked the question under his breath whenever the responsibilities felt as if they were getting too much for him. He asked it on the days when he felt there was just too much going on, too many decisions to be made, too many balls to keep in the air.

But on one level at least he was about to find that it had all been worthwhile. Out of the blue he was told that a consortium of rivals and other investors were putting together an offer for Olga TV. An offer for £24 million, which would give him a cool £13 million profit in little more than six months. As it turned out, the sale didn't go through. But the confidence boost Paul got out of knowing how valuable his new company was perceived to be was enough to see him through to the end of his new show's gruelling first series.

'Let's do it all again in September! Like cold sores, we'll be back!' As everyone said their goodbyes at the end of the run, Paul was preparing for a desperately needed summer break. He knew he needed to step back from events and take a look at how his life was turning out. He needed some space to reflect, and as he did so his thoughts, of course, kept drifting back to Brendan. The *Daily Mirror*'s Sue Carroll has long since become a friend as well as a professional contact of Paul's, and she says she nearly cried after one deeply emotional conversation with Paul that summer. Success, he told her, was now bittersweet.

'So much has happened in the months since Brendan died – what with the rows with ITV and the headlines – that my life might have begun to resemble a soap opera. But it's not a soap. It's real life and I'm still grieving. That's taken me a while to recognise. The other day I came across one of his old jumpers, there were some of his hairs on it. I had to throw it back in the wardrobe and shut the door. I can't deal with it.' Sue remembers the break in Paul's voice as he struggled to continue. When certain songs or snatches of music come on the radio he still has to turn it off, he told her, before the memories flood back and paralyse him. And he was starting to fear that he could never go back to his beloved Western Isles of Scotland, or to St Malo in northern France, where the memories of good times with Brendan were also too strong. 'Paul said he would feel like a ghost, going back to some of the places he and Murphy had visited,' Sue remembers.

With all these thoughts swirling around his head, Paul suddenly realised that a quiet, reflective summer was the last thing he needed. His peace of mind depended on him keeping busy – and fortunately there were plenty of people around offering him something to do. First up in the summer of 2006 came talk that he would replace Sue Lawley as the presenter of Radio 4's *Desert Island Discs* (when he had been a guest on the programme, Paul had picked music by Nina Simone, Elvis, Barbra Streisand and *You Gotta Have A Gimmick* from the musical *Gypsy* – the song that he, Cilla Black and Barbara Windsor had so famously performed at the *Royal Variety Performance*). Then there were rumours that he had signed to host a revived *Celebrity Squares*, and despite the bust-up with ITV there were still vague talks about him joining a new talent show with Simon Cowell.

When he wasn't in meetings about all these challenges, Paul was jotting down some thoughts for a show he wanted to appear in with Cilla. And he was already gearing up for the second series of *The New Paul O'Grady Show*. For all his claims of winging it and refusing to use a script, Paul has never turned up to work unprepared. He works hard behind the scenes – because he thinks he ought to and because he loves it.

'I don't rehearse, but I do research,' is how he describes it. 'If I've got an author on, I'll always read the book. I think that's the least you can do rather than just reading the researcher's notes. I suppose I do so much research because I really love television. That's why I work in it. I'm passionate about it and I always have been. If I watch something that's well made and interesting I am in awe of it. I've no intention of giving it all up for a long time yet.'

That's what he said in the long hot summer of 2006. But was life about to force him to do just that? Out of the blue, Paul was going to be dealt yet another terrible blow. This time he would be lucky to survive.

CHAPTER FIFTEEN

Intensive Care

Friday 30 June was supposed to be just an ordinary summer's day in the country for Paul. But on that particular Tuesday Paul was to suffer his second massive heart attack – though, amazingly, he knew very little about it at the time. 'I was in Waitrose and I remember thinking, "Has the floor moved?" I had to go and sit down surreptitiously by the cold meats. Basically, I just didn't feel well. I got home and went to lie down, I didn't even unpack the car.'

The following morning he got up, collected his shopping and went for a swim, dismissing the pain he felt in his arm and the tightening of his jaw. He says he can hardly believe it now, but later that day he decided to do some work around the house. He made some ice cream in the kitchen and lugged some heavy furniture around to make space for a DIY project. He didn't feel on top form, but he didn't feel bad enough to slow down. It was only on the Thursday night that he started to feel really ill again. At 4am on the Friday morning he woke up with a start.

'I'm having a heart attack.'

That was the first thought that went through his mind when the pain jolted him awake, then, 'Keep your cool. Don't panic. Panicking is the worst thing you can do.'

Paul lay still in bed, sweating slightly as he thought back to the pains he had felt earlier in the week, to the attack he had suffered in London four years earlier and the way both his parents had died. He tried to sleep, but couldn't, and in the end five long hours passed before his assistant Sean arrived for work at 9am.

'Run us to the hospital, would you? I've had a heart attack.' Sean stopped in his tracks and looked at his boss. He admits now that he was panicking more than Paul as he realised how serious he was being. The pair were rushed to the William Harvey Hospital in Ashford, Kent, where Paul tried desperately to make light of the situation. 'I was incensed. I was lying in that bed in Accident and Emergency. I wasn't scared, I was flaming furious! I was lying there with the oxygen mask on, going, "Don't tell me I've had another heart attack." And they said, "I'm afraid you have." The nurse had to tell me to calm down, I was so annoyed. I just thought, "Shit, not again. How can this be happening again?"'

Joking apart, Paul knew that this time things were serious. The cardiologists said he needed an immediate operation to improve the blood flow to his heart while they worked out how much other damage had been done. While Sean sat outside calling Paul's friends and family, the doctors then moved their charge to the specialist cardiac unit for the next stage of his emergency treatment. When he came round, Paul was told more about what had happened. The doctors said they could tell from the extensive damage to his heart muscles that he had indeed had a serious attack earlier in the week – and that he had carried on with what was effectively a time bomb ticking in his body. 'You're as tough as old boots,' one doctor told him.

But everyone knew Paul's luck – and his body – might not hold for much longer so he was rushed back into the cath lab for more surgery. Over the next tense three hours Paul would have eight more stents inserted into his arteries, tiny devices that work like coiled springs and keep the vessels open and the blood moving. Once more, the surgeons were able to watch the operation on the monitors above Paul's bed – and as it was wheeled into place Paul gave a groggy groan. 'I don't want to be watching this rubbish. I've seen this film before and I didn't like it first time round,' he joked weakly with the doctors before losing consciousness.

Away from the hospital, news of Paul's attack was starting to break. 'We are shocked and concerned at what has happened. Paul is still recovering and like his many fans we wish him all the best,' Channel 4 said in an official statement. Unofficially, everyone close to Paul knew that he wasn't quite at the recovery stage just yet. The doctors were still trying to work out if he needed another and even bigger operation, this time to put a defibrillator into his heart to regulate its beat for the future. But before a decision was made on this, the doctors wanted a word. And while their message was serious, they couldn't always stop smiling when they delivered it.

'Paul, every time I turn the telly on you're standing on your head or you're on the floor covered in custard or you're fighting,' the lead doctor began, shaking his head in mock resignation. And from his sick bed Paul had to admit it was true.

'Well, I'm not just interviewing someone from *Emmerdale*,' he said. 'The show is about getting stuck in. It's slapstick, it has to be.'

'But will you calm down, at least a bit?'

'I'll try.'

Outside the hospital, Paul's friends and family were being mobbed by reporters. 'It's still very serious but he is doing much better,' his friend and former personal assistant Chad Rogers told them after his first visit. 'He's sitting up and talking. He's been laughing and joking and is starting to get back to his old self.' And so he was. The World Cup was in full swing and Paul was begging the nurses to bring a television into his ward so that he could watch the key England-Portugal quarter final the following day, when he reckoned he would be strong enough to cope with the excitement. As it turned out England lost 3-1 on penalties and went out of the tournament just as Paul was discharged and sent back to his farm. And for all his jokes he was following his doctors' orders. He would be off-screen recuperating for three months – and he reckons he slept almost solidly for the first of them.

'Overwhelming exhaustion is the most common reaction to having had a second heart attack, and it normally hits you when you return home and lose the adrenaline rush that most people feel in hospital,' says cardiac specialist Gareth Thomas. 'Your heart is likely to have suffered even more damage in the second attack than in the first, so your body has even more reason to go into shut-down mode while you try and repair yourself. Best advice is just to ride it out quietly and take as long as you need for your strength to return.'

For someone like Paul this enforced slowdown was hard to face. But in the first few weeks of his recuperation he had little choice. He says even walking down his garden path to sit in the sunshine was a huge effort. And having got there and spent half an hour surrounded by roses and hollyhocks, breathing in the scent of freshly mown grass and looking out at the animals in his fields, he knew he would struggle to get back to his living room. While he wanted to hide his weakness from his friends and family he couldn't miss the worry in everyone's eyes. One more week, and I'll be fine, he kept thinking. And by the start of August he was indeed starting to get his strength back.

In the village of Aldington itself, Paul's neighbours and friends were also rallying round – often in surprising ways. Roger Allanby was typical of the tough love approach – he said that if he saw Paul with a cigarette in the village he would make him stub it out. Others were once more offering to help with his laundry and housework, and to do his shopping and cook him meals. So many people cared so much for Paul, and his eyes stung at each small act of kindness. This was not a world he wanted to leave. It was far too soon for him to say his goodbyes.

CHAPTER SIXTEEN
Back on Top

'You should see the state of me. I look terrible.' It was the end of August, 2006 and Paul was on the phone to Sara Nathan, TV Editor of the *Sun*. 'I've had so many blood tests I've got the arms of a junkie. You wouldn't even recognise me – I look more like Janis Joplin these days.' More seriously, his blood-thinning tablets were also causing problems – if he even brushed up against anything he seemed to bruise badly and a simple cut could take days to heal. The last thing he wanted to do was agree to Sarah's request for a full interview – especially if a photographer would be coming along as part of the package. But Paul knew he couldn't stay hidden away forever. He felt he owed it to all the fans who had sent cards and letters of support to show that he was back in the land of the living. And he knew that if he was to be back on television in the autumn he would have to start some promotional work soon.

'I'm going to Italy for a few days. Let's meet when I get back,' he said. And Sarah says the star looked tanned and healthy when the day came – though Paul continued to describe himself as a 'broken toy' and said his ongoing grief over losing Murphy somehow made it feel as if his second heart attack had been inevitable.

What he also told her was that he saw a new exercise regime as the best way for him to get back to his old self. There had been times since his attack when he had felt the old ghost of depression floating back. There had been times when he felt his life was on the edge of a black hole, with all the good things being sucked away. But, he said, he finally knew both how to spot the signs of depression and how to banish them. Normally a brisk walk around his fields would help him snap out of the gloom. On other low days he got back on his bike, and pedalled around the country lanes to remind himself of how beautiful life could be. Or he would tramp off around the eight-mile Saxon Shore Way where he still found some new stunning view to marvel at on each visit.

More importantly for his fans, he was also ready to exercise his brain. He started to write notes for his production team, critiquing other daytime shows, listing new ideas for his own show. For he had made up his mind. He was planning to be back in the studio as soon as possible – if only to stop his staff from winding him up.

'Paul, I'm going to put an advert in the paper. Wanted: Replacement Host for *The New Paul O'Grady Show*. No experience necessary.'

Paul looked his producer in the eye after this latest in a long line of light-hearted threats. 'Look, I've already decided to come back. You know I've never thought of really giving up work. You know I'd go insane if I did that. I'd rather hang myself than not work.'

Behind the scenes Paul was proving this point in his own very individual fashion – by dusting, vacuuming and cleaning his own bathrooms in Kent. Despite his huge fortune he still baulked against the idea of employing too many people. He needed drivers to get him around and plenty of people did work for him at home and in the studios. But he swore he would never be too grand to do at least some of his own ironing. In the long summer break of 2006, it was some of the other things he did at home which were pushing him back into the television studios. 'It's been lovely to have time for some DIY but I need to get back to work before I do too much damage to my house,' he joked to one reporter who wanted confirmation that *The New Paul O'Grady Show* would be back on screen in the autumn.

Happy to say that it would be, Paul then spent several days a week with the production team doing the usual tweaking of the format and trying hard to keep the show fresh while retaining everyone's favourite features. Paul found the meetings incredibly inspiring. He loved being in touch with some of the show's regular guests – both the famous names and the members of the public. He loved coming up with ridiculous and probably unworkable new ideas for competitions or skits. He also loved slagging off the competition – giving damning reviews of the formats he would never take on and the shortcomings of any other interviewer who came into his sights.

The original start date for the new series of the show had been pushed back three weeks to 25 September to give Paul more time to regain his strength. And as the days passed he couldn't have been more excited. The past two years had brought far more than their fair share of extraordinary highs and terrible lows. Now he just wanted to get back to doing what he did best. Surely nothing else could go wrong now?

'Buster. Come over here. What's the matter with you, little fellow?'

It was less than a week to showtime and one more crisis was still to come. Buster, the still healthy ten-year-old Shih Tzu and Bichon Frise cross who had been such a star of Paul's shows and such a source of his strength, was in trouble. Buster tried to hide it, as all dogs do, but Paul held him close as he examined his eyes. There was something very wrong – and the vets confirmed a severe infection that threatened to leave him blind.

Buster had hardly left Paul's side since his heart attack, seeming to sense that his owner needed him. It was the same comfort and protection he had tried to offer Brendan the previous year. It was why Paul loved him so much. So he was in pieces as he checked Buster into his local veterinary hospital in Kent. The dog needed some intense treatment – and to make matters worse, Paul was told he couldn't visit him for nearly a week in case it excited Buster too much and made his recovery even slower.

In London, when the autumn television schedules were announced, the papers tried to rekindle the sofa wars of the previous two years. But Paul had long since made peace with Richard and Judy and no one was rising to the bait and reviving any former hostilities in 2006. When reporters held up newer chat-show combatants like Sharon Osbourne and Brian Conley, Paul still refused to shoot them down. 'Sharon is such a smashing woman, she's really nice and she's a friend. People say we should be rivals but I don't see it that way. I've been through serious issues lately. Teatime telly is not top of the agenda,' he said, trying to draw a line under the arguments of the past.

That said, it wasn't all sweetness and light from the O'Grady camp that autumn. Some things did matter a great deal to him – and when the time was right he was still ready to speak out about them. One key issue was the way ITV was floundering amid so much competition from rival channels. 'I was brought up with ITV and it breaks my heart that it just runs repeats of *Taggart* now, and doesn't concentrate on making new shows. If they put the effort in they could be back on top again,' he said privately. Publicly he said even more. At the year's TV Quick Awards he made a pointed and sarcastic speech thanking ITV for giving him 'the last lifeboat off the *Titanic*' by letting him move to Channel 4. 'It couldn't sink any lower,' he said afterwards when he was accused of being unfair to his former employer.

In his mind, Paul's words had simply been constructive criticism. He doesn't lash out at others without good reason. And when he does speak out of turn he is always ready to apologise if he oversteps the mark. Coleen McLoughlin was a case in point that autumn. Paul had famously told her to get a job amid media claims that she simply spent her time spending Wayne Rooney's money. 'What would I say to her if I met her now? I'd tell her I'm a gobby, nosey bastard. And I'd say sorry,' he said in response to reporters' questions after learning more about Coleen's life and her efforts to earn money in her own right.

'Go out and give 'em hell.'

Once more it was time for the six words that Brendan had said in the wings before almost every performance Paul had given. Alone in his BBC dressing room that autumn, Paul had to whisper them to himself just before the first show of the new series was recorded. As he did so, he could see his old pal's face in his mind's eye with a clarity that never faded. He would give 'em hell. He would never let himself or Murphy down.

'And in five, four, three, two, one...' The warm-up had finished, the music had played and the cameras were rolling. Paul closed his eyes and took a deep breath before striding out on to the stage. The applause was incredible – Paul was being welcomed back onto television, but also being welcomed back to health. It was Monday 25 September and it was an incredibly moving moment. But that didn't mean it wasn't worthy of a typical one-liner. 'Thank you. Thank you all very, very much. It's very nice to be here. Very nice to be anywhere that doesn't have four handles and a lid.' The applause began again as Paul walked towards his now-famous desk and tried to pull this first show together.

At the start of most of his shows, he runs through a brilliant mixture of letters, messages and gifts from viewers. Sometimes there are references to previous shows, sometimes brief stories of people's lives, and frequently more canine humiliation for the long-suffering Buster, happily dressed in some wonderful new outfit sent in by a fan.

But on that Monday in September 2006 Paul had other letters in mind as he began his show. He wanted to say thank you for the extraordinary 7,000 letters of support and get well cards. And, of course, he wanted to do so with a smile. 'It's been incredible. I've had masses said for me. There are nuns and priests with repetitive strain injury. And there's been so many flowers. If it happens again, just send money.'

The jokes at his own expense continued throughout that emotional first show. His guest list was as good as ever – he had invited the usual mix of old pals and big name stars to come on board for the next five days. Barbara Windsor, Charlotte Church, Terry Wogan, Peter Kay, Ricky Tomlinson and *Desperate Housewives*' hunk Jesse Metcalfe would all sit on the sofa. With Buster still ill, Olga was there to add to the entertainment and the usual mix of audience members and variety show guests made each of the early shows a party. Everyone wanted to ask Paul how he was and every time he was ready with a quip. 'I'm fine. And my blood is so thin it should be on the cover of *Heat* magazine,' he laughed – laughing even more during a dance routine with some pearly kings and queens when one of them said, 'I thought you were dead.'

Over the next few days, Paul would find out that it wasn't just the studio audience and the production team who had welcomed him back with open arms. His overall viewing figures had hit a new peak and the critics couldn't praise him enough. 'Paul came back hitting the ground running, with his inimitable pace and wit. He easily out-did Sharon's two-part interview with David Beckham,' wrote the *Mail on Sunday*'s brilliant television critic Jaci Stephen. 'He gets funnier and funnier. The speed of his gags is breathtaking. There's nothing on which he doesn't have an opinion. The show is one of the best hours in television history.'

Early the following month Paul received more good news. Buster was fully fit and ready to go back to work. He got a standing ovation when he trotted back on to the set in front of a delighted audience, displaying the kind of star quality that Sharon Osbourne's Minnie could only dream of, according to his proud owner.

Shortly afterwards, Paul collected the Ten Years At The Top award at the TV Quick and TV Choice presentation. He had been the unanimous choice of the judges and he won the biggest cheer of the night from the audience. As usual, he still refused to take himself too seriously, though. The Avenue of the Stars was still making the news in London as the city's attempt to create a Hollywood Boulevard-style attraction – and Paul was not yet part of it. 'By the time they get to me they'll have used up all of Covent Garden and the West End and my star will be in Streatham or some other hellhole,' he joked.

Away from the bright lights of the awards ceremonies Paul's life had changed dramatically from the hell-raising days of his early career – as all his oldest friends can attest. 'When we met we wanted to out on the town partying all the time, like rock chicks,' laughs Amanda Mealing. 'Now we both have farms in the country and when we are in London together we'll go out to dinner and talk about what we are feeding our goats and what recipes we have tried recently.' They are both defying expectations, Amanda feels. 'We're growing old gracefully, not disgracefully.'

Cilla Black was next to paint a similar picture. 'I remember when Savage rang me from his farm in Kent. He'd got a sick goat in bed with him. His electricity had gone down. He was freezing. I said: "Check into a hotel, Paul." He said: "I can't. The electric gates have jammed." So he gave the goat a pill, and he had a pill, and they went to sleep. They never did that on *All Creatures Great and Small* but it's exactly what I have come to expect from Paul.'

The fact is that Paul's life today really is a long way from the celebrity-studded whirl the gossip columnists sometimes suggest. He and Cilla frequently laugh over the suggestions that they are constantly in places like The Ivy with the likes of Dale Winton and Christopher Biggins – the men dubbed 'Cilla's mafia', who supposedly pick out and vet Cilla's potential dates. In truth, Paul and Cilla do sometimes take short holidays together and love each other's company. But they don't live in each others' pockets. Paul also says he can go months if not years without ever seeing the likes of Dale and Christopher. And the regular table at The Ivy? 'Honestly, I rarely go there,' he says. 'And when I do I just want to have my food and get out.'

So were all his health scares behind him as winter approached? Doctors say that the sad truth is that when you have had two heart attacks and come from a family with such a bad history of coronary difficulties you can never properly relax. The message was reinforced that autumn when an exhausted and embarrassed Paul was told by his doctors that he had to take a week off his show to try and regain his strength. When a month later they told him he needed to do so again he was devastated. As usual, the Birkenhead bruiser hated having to let down his fans, his colleagues or his celebrity guests. He also knew that hundreds of people in his audiences booked their free seats months in advance and travelled from all parts of the country to see him record the show. He hated to disappoint them by being forced to cancel but his doctors were adamant and Channel 4 agreed. If the occasional week off in the middle of the series gave their star the energy to work through until mid-December then it was a sacrifice worth making.

And fortunately, audiences didn't feel short-changed when a line-up of guest hosts was announced. Before signing off to try and recharge his batteries in the first of the weeks off, Paul had rung some of his closest showbusiness friends to see if they would stand in for him. Old favourites including Lorraine Kelly, Jesse Metcalfe, Vernon Kay, Cilla Black and Brian Conley, all agreed to help out – though everyone was pleased when the man himself was back on set in December.

On Friday 22 he ended the week ready to wish everyone a Happy Christmas on the last show of the year. This was a show Paul had been especially determined to host, not least because he knew a whole section of the audience had been reserved for a group of very special guests: doctors, nurses and support staff from the William Harvey Hospital in Ashford, Kent who had cared for him after his heart attack. It was just one extra way he had thought of to thank them for all they had done.

After all the wild eating and drinking of Christmases past, Paul should have had a relaxed and quiet break in 2006. But he ended up being more on edge than ever – because Sharyn was due to give birth to his first grandchild on Christmas Day. After suffering a miscarriage the previous year, everyone had been on tenterhooks throughout this pregnancy and Paul had been sworn to secrecy. But this time 31-year-old Sharyn was thriving. Late on Boxing Day she gave birth to Abel, a wonderful 7lb baby boy in the Royal Women's Hospital in Liverpool. Paul, of course, was beside himself. 'I'm a glamorous granddad!' he cheered, knowing he now had one more very good reason to stay healthy and live long.

So 2007 saw a calmer Paul O'Grady emerge. It was a man who accepted that he couldn't always be superman and would have to follow doctors' orders on occasion. He put his head down and worked hard. He rode out the storms over rigged phone votes on rival shows by saying he would consider resigning if his viewers had ever been misled – and he agreed that the profits from The Organ

Game phone-in should go to charity. He also rode out a minor storm when Elton John was caught swearing on a live show – when discussing his real name with a young caller, Elton said that Reginald Dwight, 'Sounds more like a banker. Some would say wanker.' Almost blushing on his viewers' behalf Paul diffused the situation with aplomb. In the autumn of 2007, when his doctors told him to take a break again, Paul saw old pals like Ross Kemp, Shane Ritchie and Lorraine Kelly take over as guest hosts on the show. And when arch rivals Richard and Judy said they were set to quit in 2008, he got ready for a possible extension of his own ratings-topping run. Today it is a happier and more relaxed man who faces the live audience five times a week. He has finally found true contentment and peace of mind in his life and his home. He has learned to live without Brendan Murphy, his guiding light for so long, and is now able to talk honestly about love, longing and loneliness.

Always a romantic, he continues to refuse to let cynicism creep in and destroy his dreams for the future. 'Yes, I believe love can last forever. My parents were in love all their married life,' he says – throwing in the obligatory joke that the last time he fell in love at first sight was when he met little Buster. More seriously, he accepts that he may well never fall properly in love again. 'When it comes to relationships I've got very old-fashioned ideas. Pictures first. Then a meal.' No, he is not a complete monk, and yes, he has his fun, he says. But one-night-stands and sexual bravado are now off limits. And even if someone great did come along, he is brave enough to admit that he might not be ready for them. 'I don't want a partner. I hate sharing a bed and answering to anybody,' he says with total honesty. 'Living with someone would be too much compromise and I don't want that any more. I don't want to be a "we", I want to be a "me" and I want to enjoy it.' Fortunately his zest for life suggests that this shouldn't be a problem. 'I'm not one of those gay men sitting around listening to Judy Garland and moping. I hang out of car windows wolf-whistling at the builders,' he laughs. 'I have friends and I'm never lonely.' With his menagerie of animals, and a farm to run, he is never bored either. When he does have spare time he has taken to painting watercolours, though he remains wary of showing them off to too many people until he is happier with his results.

In *The Paul O'Grady Show* he also hopes he has found a platform that will pass the test of time. It is a show he hugely enjoys, a format that perfectly suits his talents. The Birkenhead schoolboy who unaccountably loved the vaudeville stars of yesteryear could never have imagined that he could have single-handedly revived the variety show tradition for the 21st century. Nor that he would have had so much fun in the process.

So while other job offers continue to come in, Paul now wants to conserve his energies and play to his strengths. There will be no more three-month, cross-country live tours, no more gruelling two-shows-a-day pantos or theatre gigs. Paul will keep on supporting his friends by appearing on their chat shows, just as they appear on his. And he will take on occasional appearances that spark his attention and make him feel alive.

But he has long since stopped working for the money. He is working for the love.

Memories of all the wild and wonderful characters he has met over the years constantly make him smile. The sailors and their wives in Birkenhead. The hard grafters who carried on the face of endless challenges – and did so with humour and dignity. The brave women he saw in courts and in care homes across the country. The anonymous figures on windswept markets. The larger-than-life personalities on south London's cabaret circuit and in the comedy clubs. The gold-plated celebrities he now meets fresh from Hollywood. It doesn't matter who they are or what they have done. If you've got the guts to put on a performance then you earn Paul's respect, even if your only audience is yourself. That's why he is so keen to give ordinary, struggling people a platform on his show. That's why he thinks vaudeville and variety shows are the best forms of entertainment and why his mission is to bring them as wide an audience as possible.

When he's asked for one word to sum up his own life Paul barely hesitates. The word is 'lucky'. Life, he says, is a journey, and he is hugely grateful for where he is from, where he has been and where he is today. He's seen it all, reckons he has done most of it and he doesn't want to stop now. 'I've lived lots of different lives,' he says.

'They weren't all easy but I've enjoyed them all and I wouldn't have missed a single day of them. Not one single day.'